Two Fingers Short

Published and printed by:

Tulsi Books (a Division of Sri Tulsi Trust)
K.K. Market, Near Sanpgaon Company ...
Mumbai - 400 ...
Phone: 022-...
e-mail: tulsibooks@gmail.com info@tulsibooks.com
web: www.tulsi...

First Printing ...

ISBN ...

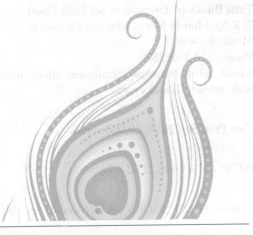

Two Fingers Short

Shubha Vilas

Published and printed by:

Tulsi Books (A Division of Sri Tulsi Trust)
7, K.M. Munshi Marg, Girgaum Chowpatty
Mumbai – 400 007
Phone: 022 23665522
e-mail: tulsibookssales@gmail.com; info@tulsibooks.com
web: www.tulsibooks.com

First Print Sep 2018: 10,000 copies

ISBN: - 978-93-81283-54-7

© 2018 TULSI BOOKS (A Division of Sri Tulsi Trust)

Contents

Contents

Acknowledgments

Walking through life, I have always seen myself as a student, surrounded by teachers who have touched and enhanced my life immensely. I would like to express my heartfelt gratitude for all that I have been fortunate enough to learn from them.

To name all of them here would be impossible; however, some of the most prominent teachers in my life have been: H.D.G. A.C. Bhaktivedanta Swami Srila Prabhupada, the founder Acarya of the Hare Krsna Movement, and H.H. Radhanath Swami, the author of the international bestseller The Journey Home – Autobiography of an American Swami and the New York Times best seller, The Journey Within.

The first chapter of this book has been inspired by the writings of HH Sivaram Maharaj, more specifically his book 'Damodar Janani'. This book has touched my heart in the most profound way. "Two Fingers Short" simply hovers over the ocean into which Sivaram Maharaj has so deeply dived. I would highly recommend all readers to read 'Damodar Janani' to understand the deepest imports of Damodar Leela.

The second chapter of this book has been inspired by a lecture of HG Sikshastakam Prabhu. Damodar

Leela from the mouth of this wonderful soul is a lot more sweeter. He has been a hero to me all my life and I silently derive a lot of inspiration from him. The fourth chapter has been inspired by a lecture of HG Gauranga Prabhu. He effortlessly makes the meaning of this highly esoteric and intense prayer so very accessible.

An attractive cover page is an essential part of every book. The credit for this innovative cover design goes to one family that took up this project so enthusiastically that I could only stand back and admire their dedication that manifested in the form of a beautiful cover page. The creativity of Dayalu Rama Prabhu, the desire of Radhika Kishori Mataji, the amazing talent of their daughter Prakriti Bharwani and the expertise of Rahul Kamath, together conceived and gave birth to "Two Fingers Short". I am eternally grateful to them for their kindness to me.

Of course, no book is complete without masterful editing and excellent proof-reading. I would like to acknowledge Dr. Shrilekha Hada and HG Shadbhuj Prabhu for doing this so expertly and painstakingly with every book of mine. This is the first book I am publishing with Tulsi Books team, which has stood by me through thick and thin. I am humbly grateful to them for everything.

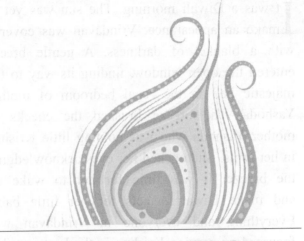

Two Fingers Short - The Story

It was a Diwali morning. The sun was yet to make an appearance. Vrindavan was covered with a blanket of darkness. A gentle breeze entered the open window, finding its way to the majestic bed in the regal bedroom of mother Yashoda. The breeze brushed the cheeks of mother Yashoda who was holding little Krishna in her arms. She opened her eyes acknowledging the breeze. It was time for her to wake up and make Diwali sweets for her little baby. Everything and everyone in Vrindavan was focussed on serving Krishna in the best possible way. She served Krishna and Vrindavan served her.

With a gentle tug, she freed herself from the little buttery arm of her baby that was tightly clutching her. Mother Yashoda got up stretching herself. It was Diwali, she remembered. A long day for her! Quickly getting ready, she walked into the kitchen of Nanda Bhavan. It wasn't a small kitchen by any standard. Hundreds of maids and servants worked there tirelessly all day long. Mother Yashoda did not need to lift a single kitchenware. There would be a dozen people ready to do anything at her beck and call. But when it came to her precious Krishna, she felt that no one could do better than what she could do as a mother. It was not about taste, it was about love.

On her list were a lot of sweets and savouries to be prepared. The only time she had was till little Krishna woke up from His transcendental slumber. Once He was awake, He would demand her constant attention. Now, that was only one side of the story! The other side was that once He woke up, there was nothing else that Yashoda preferred to do except pamper Him with her love. As she readied the kitchen for the laborious cooking that was about to happen, she glanced at the various ingredients that had been collected and stored together last evening itself. Most important on her agenda were the sweet preparations, Krishna being a sweet child with a sweet tooth. How He loved the sweets a wee bit sweeter than regular! That extra sweetness always made Him smile so sweetly. Yashoda smiled imagining His smile.

The most important ingredient, the king of her kitchen, was milk. It simply had to be the best. She gave special attention to the quality of milk, devising an elaborate ingenious process to ensure that the best of the best milk was obtained for Krishna's pleasure. Nanda Bhavan proudly housed nine lakhs beautiful cows. Of the nine lakh cows, mother Yashoda had carefully selected eight of the most robust cows who were then given special attention. These eight were fed a very special type of grass which had the fragrance of lotus flowers. This grass was known as the padma-gandha grass. Being fed with fragrant grass, the milk of these cows had the fragrance of lotus. The milk of these seven cows was then fed to the eighth cow. The milk of the eighth cow was thus the highest quality of milk in the whole of Vrindavan. Knowing that the milk would be used for Krishna, the eighth cow gave more milk than any other cow in the barn. The milk that was stored in all the urns of mother Yashoda's kitchen was the milk from that special cow!

As Yashoda turned around inspecting all the ingredients, her eyes gleamed with joy. There was intense action going on. Effortlessly gliding around the kitchen, she monitored several fires simultaneously. While several maids carried out small chores for her, she herself monitored all the fires and the delcacies being cooked on each one of them. Having set everything rolling, now it was time for her to do something that she loved and something that Krishna was mad about. Butter! She loved to churn fresh butter for Krishna every day. The butter from the Padma-gandha milk was absolutely the best in the world. She had hoped that the taste of that butter would excite Krishna so much that He wouldn't even consider the idea of stealing butter from other gopis' houses.

Drops of perspiration gathered on her forehead. Two rivers began to flow down from her brows heading towards her reddish lips. With a flick of her fingers, she diverted them and they reached her neck instead. Now mother Yashoda concentrated on the churning urn. Seated right in the middle of the kitchen, was a huge kingly urn that contained yogurt. Dipped in the middle of the thick yogurt was a wooden rod tied with a silken rope. The ends of the rope were fastened to a soft velvet cloth that acted as a soft grip for mother Yashoda to wrap her fingers around. It was almost like a warrior gripping the reins of his horse. She began to pull and push the ropes alternately causing the rod to churn the yogurt inside the urn. As she got comfortable with it, her speed increased. The churning rod whirled and swirled at the base of the earthen urn, splashing the liquidy yogurt and creating a special sound.

The musical ears of mother Yashoda caught the beat, inspiring her to churn rhythmically. Her bell shaped earrings swung into rhythm to blend into a sweet tinkle. She tapped her feet in sync with the euphonic orchestra. The silver anklets in her feet added a jingle to the symphony. The bangles on her hands were clanging along in rhythm with her hand movements. Yashoda began to sing sweet little ditties that she herself had composed. These weren't simply songs, they were memories captured in words. Every experience she had with Krishna was converted into lyrics that stayed with her for life. As she engaged herself in cooking, she sang these songs to rejuvenate her mornings. The maids would eagerly make note of the new compositions and by evening every resident of Vrindavan had these songs on their lips.

Dressed in a saffron sari, perched on a small wooden stool, mother Yashoda was busy using her words in glorifying Krishna, her mind in recollecting the divine pastimes of Krishna and her hands in actively serving Krishna. The malati flowers on mother Yashoda's hair were embarrassed to be sitting on the head of such an exalted personality, preferring to reside at her feet. One by one they began to drop themselves at her feet. When her maids saw her in this posture, they felt that they were in presence of a sanyasi whose body mind and words were fully engaged in serving the Lord.

Suddenly everything came to a standstill! The rod stopped churning. The anklets stopped jingling. The bangles stopped clanging. The earrings stopped swinging. Yashoda stopped singing. As if time had frozen in that one moment. It was the moment mother Yashoda saw the beautiful face of little Krishna standing in front of her, snatching the churning rod with His cute little fingers. Whenever she saw her darling son Krishna, everything around her froze.

The melodious singing of mother Yashoda's devotional ecstasies had reached sleeping Krishna's ears, dragging Him out of His transcendental slumber. Fighting against the desperation to sleep and hungry to experience mother Yashoda's love, Krishna crawled out of His bed on His stomach and somehow lowered Himself onto the floor. Crawling quickly from the bedroom into the kitchen, Krishna yearned to see His mother. On seeing her immersed in the churning activity, He crawled on His fours towards her. His mother's eyes were closed, blissfully absorbed in singing songs of her wonderful memories. For a moment Krishna smiled admiring the breath taking beauty of His mother's love. The very next moment He frowned, annoyed at her for paying so much attention to a pot of yogurt while neglecting her sleeping child.

Yashoda looked at her darling son standing on his legs holding the churning rod with one hand and the end of her sari with the other hand. His eyes were fiery red, glaring at her as if saying 'stop this churning business and feed Me'. The all-knowing mother smiled. Her child was hungry. Hungry for her love. Letting go of the ropes connected to the churning rod, she held out her arms. Krishna rushed into her outstretched arms. As she placed little Krishna on her lap, there was a beautiful smile of contentment on His divine face as He relished the nectar of His mother's love.

Just as she was happily gazing at her darling drink milk with great joy, a smell caught her attention. Unmistakably, it was the smell of milk boiling over. The strong smell was followed by a crackling sound of milk spilling out of the vessel. Mother Yashoda frantically placed Krishna on the ground, and ran over to the stove where the milk was. When the choice was between serving Krishna with her milk or serving Krishna by saving the precious Padma-gandha milk that was boiling over, she chose to save the milk from which she had planned to make so many milk confectioneries.

While Yashoda had been busy feeding Krishna with her milk, the milk that was on the stove was worried. It was well known that Yashoda's love for Krishna was unlimited, therefore the quantity of her milk was also unlimited and Krishna's ability to drink that milk was also unlimited. Given this scenario, the scope for it to serve Krishna was extremely limited. The milk came to the conclusion that if there was no scope for serving Krishna in this life, then there was no point in continuing to live. Better to commit suicide by jumping into the cooking fire below the vessel! Thus it decided to boil over and end its wasteful existence.

As mother Yashoda busied herself in taking care of the boiling milk vessel and then in cleaning the spilt milk portion on the stove, Krishna was grinding His teeth in sheer anger. He bit His red lips with His pearly white teeth. The contrast between the colors of his teeth and lips was just as stark as the contrast between his sweet personality and His extreme anger. His eyes brimmed with tears. He clenched His fists in utter frustration. How could she do this to Him? For mere two litres of milk, she had left Him high and dry? Just when He had begun to relish her love, she had dumped Him to attend to something as insignificant as milk boiling over. This was totally unacceptable!

Resenting the interruption in His enjoyment, He looked around for something that could be used to teach her a lesson. In one corner of the room He found exactly what He was looking for, a pestle stone. It was inviting Krishna excitedly. Krishna ran upto it, picked it up and returned to the churning urn. He glared at the urn with great vengeance in His eyes. This was his enemy number one! Mother had given it all her attention in the morning while neglecting Him. Hitting hard at the base, He broke the urn creating a hole there. Liquid yogurt and the newly-formed butter flowed out rapidly. In a matter of seconds, there was a puddle of butter at the base of the urn which slowly crawled towards Krishna's feet. This was just the beginning! He had more to do to teach His mother an unforgettable lesson - not to neglect Him when He so badly wanted her.

His eyes darted towards the store house, the next target of His wrath. But to reach the storehouse and plunder it, there was a big hurdle He had to cross. Right at His feet was a huge puddle that had formed. Without crossing that puddle, He wouldn't be able to reach the store. He wasn't confident that His little legs would actually jump across the puddle. He could try. He took a step back and jumped across. Though He did His best, His little feet landed right in the middle of the puddle creating a splash. Krishna sighed and shrugged His shoulders. He couldn't wait there anymore, He had important things to take care of. He began to run as fast as He could, towards the storehouse. As He ran, little white footprints were etched on the floor leaving a cute trail behind.

As soon as Krishna stepped into the storeroom, He grinned a naughty grin. An unlimited scope for mischief awaited Him here! One by one He brought down all the pots that were stored in the room. His eyes sparkled at the sight of all the goodies. He tasted a little from each pot, and then flung the rest on the walls and onto the floor. Very soon, all the walls of the storeroom were splattered with butter, milk and curd. Finally after crashing all the empty pots on the ground, He left. Taking along one pot of butter with Him.

When mother Yashoda came back after taking care of the kitchen duties that needed her immediate attention, a royal mess awaited her. She was shocked to see the damage Krishna had done to her hard work. How hadn't she heard any noise? Though angry she smiled weakly, thinking about her little son's well developed intelligence and presence of mind. He had hit the base of the earthen urn fully aware that the urn was filled with yogurt and hitting at the base would cause the least amount of noise and the maximum damage. She followed the buttery footprints of Krishna, wondering where they would lead her. She found herself inside the storehouse where a much bigger chaos was waiting to greet her. A shrill scream escaped her mouth at the crime scene!

All the maids at once dropped everything they were doing and rushed to the storehouse. They got a shock of their lives when they saw the horrifying mess in the storeroom. Mother Yashoda, seated on a small stool, stared blankly at the messy patterns splashed on one particularly ruined wall. Suddenly her mood changed from despondency to rage. She was no more the housewife worried about her vandalized household but an angry mother who was determined to discipline her naughty son. Picking up a bejewelled stick from a corner of the kitchen cabinet, Yashoda set out on a mission to track down the prankster and punish Him suitably.

Following the small footprints of Krishna that exited the storeroom, she reached her backyard. As she peeped out of the window that gave a clear vision of the backyard, she saw something that was further unbelievable. Her little Krishna was standing on top of an unused upside-down grinding mortar and addressing a group of chattering monkeys who were greedily eyeing the butter pot in His hands. He then sat down cross-legged on the grinding mortar and began to toss chunks of butter towards them. The monkeys were so excited that their chattering knew no bounds. They happily ate every bit of the butter that came their way and waited for more.

Mother Yashoda was furious at her son's increasingly delinquent acts. So much effort went into making fresh hand-churned butter for Krishna and here He was wasting it away on reckless monkeys. Yashoda bolted towards the garden with the stick in her hand. Krishna's back was towards her. He had no idea of the fast approaching calamity. However there was a sudden change in the facial expressions of the monkeys. A moment ago, they were all smiling and happy eating the soft tasty butter being offered to them so generously. The next moment their eyes were full of panic not knowing where to look. They had the look of innocent children caught in a naughty act. The sudden change of expression alerted Krishna. In fact, in the eyes of one of the monkeys He saw His mother approaching. He suddenly realized what that meant. He turned around just in time to see mother Yashoda rushing towards Him with a mean-looking stick raised high above her head.

Instantly dropping the butter pot from His lap, Krishna stood up on the grinding mortar and jumped on to the ground. His delicate feet wobbled with the impact of the jump and He almost lost His balance. One glance behind was enough to remind Him that there was no time for recovery. He had to save Himself anyhow from that mean looking stick in His mother's hand. He ran for His life. He couldn't help thinking as He ran, how much His mother had changed since morning. She was always so loving and caring. But now the mean look she had while chasing Him with that stick made her unrecognizable. He felt all alone, having to protect Himself from His own mother. Little Krishna fled with all the speed He could muster. He had never known the meaning of fear in His life until now. But the stick in His mother's hands and the angry look on her face had initiated Him into the world of fear.

Mother Yashoda ran after Him with great speed, more out of love than out of anger. That little boy had actually jumped from the wooden grinding mortar. She had noticed His legs wobble from the impact of the jump. Her heart had reached out to Him. But she realized that He was too frightened to even look at her. There were two voices simultaneously speaking inside her. One was the voice of a loving mother who was very concerned about her son. Concerned about His fearful condition at the sight of the stick in her hand. Second was the voice of a strict disciplinarian who couldn't tolerate the morning's disruptive behaviour of a naughty prankster. One voice told her to throw the stick away and embrace the scared child. The second voice told her to not to melt but punish Him so that He doesn't dare repeat the unacceptable behaviour.

As mother Yashoda was fighting with the two voices within her head, there were two more voices on top of her head that were arguing too. These were the voices of the flowers on her hair that had divided themselves into two teams. Some of the flowers were supporting Krishna and the others were in support of mother Yashoda. Those supporting Krishna were totally against mother Yashoda's stern inhuman action. How could she scare a little delicate child like Him? Those supporting mother Yashoda argued that she could never be wrong because whatever she did was out of her love for Krishna. It was high time Krishna was given some disciplining.

The flowers supporting mother Yashoda decided that they would support her in every possible way. The best way to do that was to decrease her burden. Even if they could reduce the burden on her body by a fragment, they would have contributed to her mission of catching Krishna. Concluding thus, all the flowers on mother Yashoda's team jumped off her head, decreasing her burden and increasing her speed.

The flowers supporting Krishna decided that they would not want to be connected to mother Yashoda in anyway whatsoever. Why should they have even a remote connection with anyone against Krishna? If Krishna saw them on Yashoda's head, He would surely get furious with them and question their loyalty. The best way to show their loyalty was to stay far away from Yashoda. Concluding thus, all the flowers on Krishna's side jumped off her head, wanting to show Krishna that they have no connection with her whatsoever.

Without the burden of flowers on her head, Yashoda's speed increased considerably and she caught up with Krishna very soon. Grabbing his arm, Yashoda pulled him towards herself, stopping Him in His tracks. The uncatchable was caught. Both, mother and son were panting hard. Bending forward, both of them took a few seconds to catch their breath. For Krishna there were more things to worry about. The most worrisome thing was the fearsome stick in His mother's hand. As she held his arms tightly with one hand preventing him from running away, the stick on the other hand kept coming menacingly closer to Krishna's face. His eyes were transfixed on that dancing stick. His lips began to tremble and tears began to roll down His cheeks dragging along with them the black maskara in His eyes. With His free hand, He began to rub His teary eyes adding further to the mess His running tears had already created on His face. Soon His entire body was heaving while He sobbed uncontrollably.

Sensing that the stick had caused such anxiety in her little child, mother Yashoda dropped the stick instantly. The child was in great fear.

He was also in great anger. If she let Him go now with such a disturbed mind then surely He would not only cause more damage but could potentially harm Himself. Plus, she also had a lot of work to do and couldn't afford to spend more time trying to keep Him away from mischief.

She resolved to do something that would help achieve all goals at once. Something that would prevent Him from cooking up more trouble; something that would act as a punishment, acting as a reminder every time He thinks of doing something as naughty; something that would act as a tranquilizer to allow Krishna a chance to calm His currently agitated mind; and something that would give her space to do her activities without having to bother about her son getting into trouble. Phew!

As she looked around trying to find a suitable solution that would take care of all these agendas, her eyes fell on exactly what she was looking for. The very thing that was His partner in crime would be His partner in punishment now. Mother Yashoda had spotted an unused grinding mortar lying in the corner of the roadway. That was her solution.

In the process of outrunning mother, Krishna had reached outside the palace gates of Nanda Bhavan. He had surmised that His mother may slow down and in fact let go of the chase in public eye. But that was far from what happened. She in fact, increased her speed and caught Him in full public view. A small crowd of onlookers had gathered around the mother-son duo. It was no more a mother-son private affair. Yashoda dragged Krishna to that mortar. Krishna panicked as He realized her humiliating intention. How could His mother subject Him publically to such humiliation? He was as embarrassed as she was determined.

She couldn't loosen her hold on Him even for a moment. But she also needed to fetch a rope to tie Him up to the grinding mortar. It was a tricky situation for the mother. Suddenly she hit upon an idea. The idea was right on top of her head. Literally! She decided to use the ribbon that held her hair plaits to tie up Krishna. Not too sure if the length of the ribbon was enough to tie His waist, she decided to try it. As expected, it wasn't enough. It was falling two fingers too short. She then untied the silken rope that was holding together the end of her braid. Tying the two silken ribbons together, she then tried to bind Krishna. Surprisingly, the addition made no difference; she was still falling short by two fingers. She saw her maids gather around from the household and sent them to get more rope to tie her naughty son. The maids ran into the house and returned quickly with few more ropes. They managed to get all the ropes that were used for churning butter. Since they knew that these ropes were going to tie Krishna's belly, they selected the softest ones. Expertly tying together all the ropes available in a sequence, mother Yashoda tried tying up Krishna once again. Oh, how disappointing! The combined rope was falling short by exactly two fingers distance once again! Mother Yashoda was quite bewildered by the unexplainable phenomenon. But she decided not to give up so easily.

While everyone around was utterly surprised by the miraculous events unfolding in front of them, Krishna stared at the ground not wanting to see anyone. He was too embarrassed for words with an audience witnessing His mother tying Him in the open.

She ordered the maids to get as many ropes as they could from the household. They soon returned armed with a huge number of ropes. Practically every string or cloth that was used to hang the pots of butter, milk, yogurt and everything else was roped in. The gopis began to assist mother Yashoda in binding the ropes together securely. After all the ropes were tied together, mother Yashoda then cast the rope around Krishna's belly to tie Him to the grinding mortar. And guess what? The combined rope again fell short by just two fingers. How could that be?

A whisperous roar erupted from the crowd as everyone tried to make sense of the mystical event they were witnessing. The Diwali festival was long forgotten. Vrindavan was celebrating another festival. This was the rope festival. Mother Yashoda ordered all the gopis to go to the cowshed and get all the ropes from there. The gopis ran with great enthusiasm to Nanda Maharaj's cowshed. There were nine lakh cows and each of them had ropes attached to them. The gopis untied all the ropes and gathered them together in big heaps. Soon they were carrying hundreds of thousands of ropes to the scene where the mother and son were exhibiting their determination. Krishna was determined to resist being bound and Yashoda was determined to overcome any resistance to her desire of binding Krishna. As the villagers of Vrindavan saw mother Yashoda struggling to tie up all those thousands of ropes to make a huge ropeline, they felt sorry for her and began to advise her to forget her desire to tie Krishna. Some said that God didn't want little Krishna to be tied up that day. There was no point in trying to go against the will of nature. One glare from mother Yashoda was enough to shut their mouths. She was His mother and her duty was to discipline her child. What was God's role in this matter? Even if God didn't want her to tie up Krishna, she was going to do it anyway. Whatever it took to do that. With nine lakh ropes being bound together along with the rest of the ropes already there, there was hardly any scope of not being able to bind Krishna, irrespective of what God wanted.

Happy with her handiwork, mother Yashoda placed the rope around Krishna's waist and once again tried to bind Him by placing that final knot. Lo and behold, once again two fingers too short! The entire length of that combined rope had shrunk and the rope was falling two fingers short like the original rope. Yashoda was flabbergasted. Shocked beyond belief! How did that happen? How was it possible? Krishna's waist hadn't even increased in size. In fact it only seemed to have decreased a bit due to hunger. Mother Yashoda had been in this rope tying business all the way from morning till afternoon now. Practically half the day had gone by tying rope after rope. In fact the entire area had been filled with ropes of all colors and shapes and sizes. Now all those ropes had disappeared and the combined rope was equally small. After such a lot of effort, the result was exactly the same! But every disappointment only made her determination stronger. Finally, she asked all the Vrajvasis to go home and bring as many ropes as they could.

The Vrajvasis were thrilled to know that they were also going to be a part of this incredible pastime. They sped home and gathered every rope they could lay their hands on. Soon every rope in the whole of Vrindavan was lying at Mother Yashoda's feet. She and her maids immediately got into action. They tied each and every rope together thus making one huge ropeline. The whole process took so long that afternoon had merged into evening. They had begun at day break and now it was almost sun set. Mother Yashoda's determination to bind Krishna hadn't decreased one bit. For the Vrajvasis, now it was no more about binding Krishna, rather it was about being with Krishna all day. They happily helped her tie the ropes together, while simultaneously glancing at Krishna. Krishna sat near the grinding mortar enjoying the struggle that mother Yashoda was going through to bind Him. He would even break into a naughty smile when mother was too engrossed to look at him. As soon as she looked towards Him, He would lower his eyes, feigning sadness at being punished like this.

Finally when all the ropes were tied up, mother Yashoda walked towards Krishna to make a last attempt of tying Him up yet again. By this time there were hundreds of onlookers. The news had spread and everyone wanted to see the magic phenomenon for themselves. What was fun for the Vrajvasis had been hard work for mother. She was dripping with sweat. As she threw the rope behind Krishna and tried to bring the two ends of the rope together, it happened yet again. The rope was two fingers too short again! When it happened this time, all the onlookers let out a loud sigh!

That was it! Krishna can't be tied. Mother Yashoda was wanting to do the impossible. They had already warned her right in the beginning. While everyone was discussing the impossibility of tying Krishna, there was something special happening between the mother and the son. A drop of sweat from mother Yashoda's body had fallen on Krishna. As soon as that happened, Krishna's heart melted. He suddenly felt compassion for His mother. All the pent up anger evaporated as soon as that drop of sweat fell on Him. Exactly at that time a little hand emerged in between Krishna and Yashoda. The hand was holding a silk ribbon. It was a soft, delicate and fragrant hand. Both mother and son turned simultaneously to see whose beautiful hand that was. It was little Radha! She had come running to contribute to the rope festival by offering the ribbon from her hair. Unfortunately, by the time she reached, everyone told her it was all over. But she was determined to help mother Yashoda tie Krishna. When mother Yashoda saw the ribbon in Radha's hand, she took it and tied it to the rope and attempted the impossible once again.

By now, Krishna's resistance had melted into the pot of His mother's determination and Radha's love. The little drop of sweat from His mother's forehead and the little ribbon from Radha's hair had done what millions of ropes from all of Vrindavan could not do. Krishna allowed Himself to be bound. When mother Yashoda tried to tie the knot almost expecting it to be two fingers too short, she was pleasantly surprised when it was a perfect fit and she was actually able to tie up Krishna. As soon as the knot was tied, she shouted joyfully. "Damodar!" Krishna now had a new name. Damodar, the one who is bound at the belly. As everyone began to shout 'Damodar, Damodar', no one was actually able to believe what had just happened. Gopis who were close to Radha muttered under their breath it was not just Damodar but Radha Damodar, the one whose belly is bound by Radha's love.

The impossible had become possible. Krishna was finally bound. As soon as the knot was tied, something even more amazing happened. The millions of ropes that had been used to tie up Krishna since morning and had mysteriously shrunk to merge into one rope that would always fall short, reappeared miraculously and fell in a heap at Krishna's feet as soon as the final knot was tied. Only the original ribbon of mother Yashoda's hair remained tying Krishna's belly with the grinding mortar. Krishna smiled at His mother. Yashoda kissed her son lovingly. Then feigning strictness she told Him that now she needed to go and clean up the mess He had created in the morning and also prepare for the Diwali festival. She warned Him not to do anything naughty while she was away and stay away from His friends. Krishna nodded His head like any obedient child.

Yashoda stood up allowing all the Vrajvasis to see the success of her endeavor. Who said she cannot discipline her child if she wants? Who said a mother's will is in anyway lesser than God's will? With tears in their eyes, all the Vrajvasis saw their little darling tied up helplessly to the grinding mortar. Mother Yashoda then addressed all the onlookers requesting them to return home and attend to their duties. Enough time had been wasted since morning and all of them had to do so much to ready themselves for the festivities that were about to begin. Soon the whole crowd dispersed talking about the day's mystical activities. Yashoda had another song to compose about her son's pastimes. But before that she had to cook a feast and clean a big mess. Assuming that Krishna was done with doing mischief for the day, mother Yashoda along with her maids began to focus on the work at hand. They only had a few hours to complete a whole day's work.

Once the crowd dispersed, Krishna was left alone. After all the attention He had received since morning, the silence and loneliness felt strange. It was twilight now. Vrindavan's beauty at its peak. Krishna glanced at the setting sun and the beautiful twilight sky overhead. The colors were mesmerizing. In the midst of orangish red clouds, the most powerful demigods in creation had gathered together to discuss Krishna's pitiable situation. They were shocked at the way the creator of the material and spiritual worlds had been treated in Vrindavan. How could they tie up the Supreme Personality of Godhead? Moreover, they wondered, why would Krishna allow Himself to be tied up like that?

Krishna smiled at their confusion. With hands raised towards the sky, He declared to the demigods what would remain etched in their minds forever. He revealed that at present, He had the highest position He could ever have. The position of being tied up by His devotee's love. The pleasure He experienced in being bound by His mother's love was higher than the highest pleasure of the spiritual world; nothing could equal that. He further declared that the only purpose of His appearance in Vrindavan was to show the world that He was a slave of His pure devotees' love.

The demigods had a vast amount of knowledge stored in their heads, but this knowledge that

Krishna shared with them was higher than anything else they had heard so far. Their heads spun as they tried to filter the extent and depth of what Krishna had revealed to them. They offered their obeisances to Damodar, who was bound by His mother's pure love, and then dispersed. Vrindavan was too complex to comprehend!

Just as the demigods made their exit, a group of monkeys surrounded Krishna. The very monkeys whom He had fed butter that morning and was caught in the act. They had sorry faces; wanting to help but clueless about how to help. The only thing they could do was make funny monkey faces and make Him laugh and forget His worries. The next moment, Krishna's best friends appeared to entertain Krishna and give Him company. They tried to untie Him. But no matter how much they tried, it was impossible to untie the knot tied by Yashoda. The knot seemed too complex for His friends to handle. They gave up finally. They had to help Him in other ways. Was He feeling hungry?

Krishna immediately realized that He was; He hadn't eaten anything since morning. Soon He masterminded another robbery. He instructed His friends to steal the best of eatables from their own houses and get for Him. Within no time, the boys were all seated together around Krishna and having a royal picnic. Krishna even forgot that He was still bound to the mortar as He laughed and joked with His friends, eating sumptuous butter, yogurt and other preparations His friends had managed to sneak out.

Once He had eaten to contentment, He thought about His next move. He looked around and His eyes were drawn towards two huge trees popularly called Yamala Arjuna trees. He pushed the mortar to see how heavy it was. After gauging its weight, He tugged at it. It fell horizontally. Now it could roll on its own with a little tugging. He began to tug at the grinding mortar with His head facing the twin trees. His friends were confused - what was Krishna trying to do? Wouldn't mother Yashoda throw a tantrum if He moved away from the spot where she had tied Him? Krishna surely knew how to get more and more entangled in difficult situations. They wanted to run along with Krishna but some mystical potency kept their feet rooted to the ground. It was almost as if a mysterious force had immobilized them.

Krishna crawled on His hands and knees with the grinding mortar following his movements. He squeezed past the gap between the two trees but the mortar got stuck in between them. Krishna yanked the mortar trying to free it. No luck. He applied more force to dislodge the stuck mortar. Nothing happened. He continued to put in more effort, and suddenly the two huge trees began to shake. As He tugged harder, there was a huge sound. The two trees toppled over from the base resulting in an ear-splitting crash. Krishna was stationed right in between the trees and even though the trees lunged towards Him, He was in no danger. Not a splinter touched Krishna. Out of the two fallen trees, emerged two divine personalities. With folded hands these divine beings offered their prayers to Krishna.

The two beings were Nalakuver and Manigriva, the sons of Kuvera, the treasurer of the demigods. They paid their obeisance to Krishna and expressed gratitude for liberating them, "Twenty thousand years ago, we were bathing in the Mandakini Ganga of the heavens, intoxicated not only with varuni, the celestial beverage but also with great pride. Completely naked and in the company of girls, we were totally oblivious to the presence of Narada Muni, the divine saint. The compassionate saint wanted to purify us and help us rid of our pride. Comprehending that just bathing in the Ganga wasn't purifying enough, he cursed us to become trees in the earthly realms. Since we loved to be naked, the body of trees was deserving. When we begged sincere forgiveness, he was even more compassionate and tweaked the curse for our benefit. He predicted that we would be embodied as trees in Vrindavan where one day You would release us from the curse. We have been standing here as trees in the courtyard of Nanda Maharaj since 20,000 years simply waiting for this day when

Your auspicious glance falls on us. Today as You were bound by Your mother, You felt our pain of being bound as trees and set us free. Even in Your bound state You can liberate others."

Krishna did not bother to look at them but continued playing with the mortar as the demigods offered their serious gratitude. Finally He requested them to return to their guru Narada who would grant the fulfilment of all their desires. If it wasn't for Narada's desire, He would not have glanced in their direction. But He was bound to fulfil the words spoken by His devotees. He then turned away to look for His friends through the foliage of the fallen trees. The demigods understood that they were no more needed here and Krishna wanted His privacy. They offered their respects and returned to their heavenly abodes.

Meanwhile, Krishna's friends had been watching everything that transpired. Though they could see, they could not move even an inch as they were immobilized. As soon as the two beings left, their immobility also disappeared. They ran towards Krishna who was not in their vision, hidden as He was by the dense fallen foliage. When they finally reached the trees, they saw to their relief Krishna happily playing with the mortar.

The whole of Vrindavan had heard the tumultuous noise that had just occurred. The elder gopas and gopis immediately ran towards the source of the noise. They knew it originated from Nanda Bhavan. They also knew that Krishna was in the courtyard of Nanda Bhavan and couldn't help but worry about Him.

They were shocked to see the two huge trees fallen. How could such gigantic trees fall on their own? But their greater anxiety was that Krishna was missing from the spot where Yashoda had tied Him to the grinding mortar. They began to panic as they couldn't locate Him anywhere. Nanda Maharaj had arrived by then and he joined the search party. Krishna had made His friends hide within the foliage just to make things more dramatic. After all, what was the joy in finding something valuable without a little anxiety in searching for it? Just then mother Yashoda arrived at the scene. As soon as Krishna saw His mother, He couldn't stay hidden anymore. He instinctively stood up and everyone noticed Him. Nanda Maharaj ran up to his son and embraced Him tightly.

Chaos and disorder erupted all around as everyone began questioning the boys eagerly all at once. What exactly happened? How did the huge trees fall on their own? Where was Krishna then? The boys explained animatedly all that had transpired. The more they spoke, the more the villagers broke into smiles. The boys were confused. Why was everyone smiling unreasonably? They were talking seriously. Were the Vrajvasis thinking they had made up these stories? Indeed, the Vrajvasis believed everything they said was fiction, a product of their imagination. How could they be frozen physically and have only eye movement? How could Krishna drag down two huge trees with the help of a grinding mortar? How could gods appear from within the trees? Why would the gods offer prayers to a little child? Everything they said was simply a fairy tale stemming from their fertile brains.

The boys resigned themselves to silence when no one actually believed them. Nanda Maharaj then asked Krishna to explain how He happened to be tied up to a grinding mortar and who dared to tie up his darling son. When He heard His father's angry words, He found the opportunity of getting even with His mother. He told Nanda Maharaj about the humiliating way in which His mother tied Him to the grinding mortar for no valid reason. Nanda Maharaj glared at Yashoda for reprimanding Krishna. He in fact chastised her severely. Krishna embraced His father telling Him that His only shelter in Vrindavan was His father now. Nanda untied the weeping Krishna and carried Him in his arms. Nanda lovingly took his son to the Yamuna river and bathed Him to purify Him of the whole day's sweat and grime that had gathered over His body.

The Diwali celebrations soon began in Vrindavan. Vrindavan shone brilliantly with millions of lamps lit all over. Krishna played with His friends happily. He refused to look at Yashoda the entire evening. Mother Yashoda felt hurt and miserable ignored by her own loving son. Everything she did was out of love for her darling son. She never imagined that her act could put Krishna's life in danger. In hindsight, she felt tying Krishna was a mistake and she felt extreme remorseful about it.

All evening Krishna revelled in the company of Nanda Maharaj. He claimed that from now on He was only His father's son. After the celebrations, Nanda Maharaj realized that Yashoda was in a bad shape being denied her son's association. Something had to be done quickly to shake Krishna out of His angry mood. There was only one way to do it and that would be to bring out Krishna's intense love for His mother through an emotional outburst. Nanda Maharaj called Krishna and told Him that since he was the king of Vrindavan and as a king his duty was to punish all offenders. Since Yashoda had done the gravest offense, it was his duty to punish her in the most severe way. The very thought of His mother being punished agitated Him greatly. His mind became numb with the thought of pain of punishment for mother Yashoda. He began to wail and shout. He told Nanda Maharaj that mother Yashoda should never be punished. He ran to His mother and jumped into her arms as if protecting her from Nanda Maharaj's punishment. Yashoda was so touched by her son's love for her. Tears began to flow profusely from her eyes. Finally the mother and son were united again in love. She put Him on her lap and began to feed Him her milk once again. Krishna immediately became peaceful. Only the love of His mother could satisfy Him. Everything else in this world was nothing compared to the love that mother Yashoda showered on Him.

While the world celebrates Diwali as a festival of lights, in Vrindavan it is the festival of love. While the world remembers the return of Rama to Ayodhya on Diwali, Vrindavan remembers the return of Krishna to His mother's arms on

Diwali. Mother Yashoda conquered Krishna with her love. Krishna conquered the world with love that He experienced from His mother. All day she struggled to tie Him with a rope to bind His belly. She did manage to do it finally which earned Him the name Damodar. But much after that when she tied His belly with her arms that was when Krishna felt completely bound. Now He was aptly called Yashoda Damodar, the one bound in His belly by Yashoda.

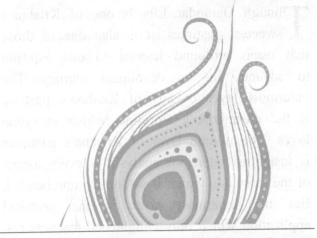

Two Fingers Short - Hidden Gems

Though Damodar Lila is one of Krishna's sweetest pastimes, it is also one of those that teach profound lessons to one aspiring to advance in the devotional journey. The outermost layer of any of Krishna's pastime is the mesmerizing storyline, which everyone loves. The middle layer of Krishna's pastimes is insightful sagacious analysis of every aspect of the storyline, which is seldom comprehended. But the innermost layer is the practical application which only enlightened teachers can decipher and help others live a meaningful life based on that.

In Vrindavan, everyone's love for Krishna goes beyond themselves. In fact they love Him so much that His Godhood gets buried deep within the mountain of their love. Even when Krishna wants to talk openly about His Godhood, no one gives it much importance. They love Him so much that they don't care if He is God. Their primary relationship with Him as a friend, son or lover is more important than their secondary relationship with Him as their creator and controller. Here is a beautiful story that illustrates just that.

It was just another day and Krishna was playing in the forest with His friends. Of the plethora of games that they played, one game they loved immensely was wrestling. Dividing themselves into two teams, they allotted opponents for the wrestling match. Sridama was chosen to wrestle with Krishna. Just to gain an advantage over His opponent by creating a fear factor, Krishna asked Sridama a question, "Do you know who I am?" Sridama smiled and boasted, "In the whole universe, if there is anyone who knows Krishna the most, it is I." Krishna ignored his friendly sarcasm and continued seriously, "I am the Supreme Personality of Godhead."

When His friends giggled and laughed at His statement, Krishna thought it was high time He gave them tangible proof to validate His claim. He said, "Don't you know that I killed Putana when I was just a six day old baby? I killed Aghasur and saved everyone from the venomous snake's mouth. And the whole of Vrindavan witnessed how I held the Govardhan hill on the little finger of My left hand for seven days and seven nights."

Everyone began to roll on the ground and laugh loudly. Sridama spoke in a mocking tone, "O Supreme Lord, let me clear your misconceptions. When the evil Putana kidnapped You, it was mother Yashoda who requested many pure brahmanas to recite powerful mantras. Their collective power was what killed Putana. As far as Your claim of killing Aghasur is concerned, let me tell you that even before You entered the snake-demon's mouth, all of us were inside and had already managed to slice him up. You entered after everything was over and simply took the credit. And as far as the lifting of Govardhan hill is concerned, everyone knows that after we worshipped the hill, it was so happy that it was floating in the air. You simply put Your finger below the hill and claimed that You were the one lifting it."

Krishna was totally dumbstruck hearing Sridama's counter claims in proving Him false.

Though He acted disturbed externally, He was joyful internally. This was exactly what He wanted to experience in Vrindavan. Love! Untinged by any element of awe and reverence. The whole universe had complete knowledge of His Godhood and acknowledged His prowess. But Vrindavan reveled in His love alone.

Once in a while, Krishna did exhibit His Godhood more openly to a select few personalities in Vrindavan. Only for a split second though. He would immediately retract His display of Godhood and resume His role as the innocent, sweet darling boy of Vrindavan. When some of His friends complained to mother Yashoda about Krishna eating mud, she inspected His mouth to check for herself. Within Krishna's tiny mouth, Yashoda saw the whole creation. In fact she even saw the village of Vrindavan and within Vrindavan she saw herself looking into Krishna's mouth. The next moment Krishna withdrew the scene and all she saw was specks of dirt dotting her naughty child's mouth.

Exalted teachers explain that behind these

sweet looking pastimes are some deep insights. The purpose of Krishna's appearance in the material realm was to reduce the burden of the earth by ridding it off the demoniac elements. When Krishna was five years old, He began to meditate on the purpose of His advent. He reflected that in the five years He had been on Earth, He had done close to nothing to reduce her burden. He wanted to begin immediately. With that purpose in mind, He picked up a handful of mud from the Earth and ate it up. He was happy thinking that He had begun His task by reducing that much burden for the time being at least.

For a child, the greatest pleasure lies in getting the mother's attention. Krishna too did so many things for His mother's attention. Of all things that children do, what catches the mother's attention is her child doing something wonderful and special. Krishna wanted to get His mother's attention by doing something like that. So He decided to show her something as wonderful as the whole creation within His mouth. But the reaction He got from her was contrary to what He had expected.

Instead of appreciating the amazing scene He had showed her, she was stunned believing her child to be the Supreme Lord. When Krishna saw His mother showing awe and reverence instead of love, He realized that His plan had backfired. Instead of getting showered with intimate love, He was getting informal worship. He immediately withdrew the vision of His universal form from inside His mouth and replaced it something that angered her.

In order to completely undo the effect of this divine vision on her mind, Krishna enacted the Damodar Lila. In the memorable Damodar Lila, Yashoda gets a chance to tie Krishna with ropes. He wanted to convince her in a logical way that if she can tie Him up with ropes, then He couldn't possibly be God. How could anyone tie God with ordinary ropes?

In addition, there were three more reasons why Krishna enacted the Damodar Lila. The first reason was that Krishna wanted to increase mother Yashoda's fame. Yashoda means one who brings "yash" or fame to Krishna. Krishna in turn wanted to bring fame for her. Most other Vedic festivals are celebrated for a day in memory of one pastime of the Lord. But the Damodar Lila is the only festival that is celebrated for an entire month. A single pastime being celebrated for an entire month! In other words, a full month dedicated to the greatness of mother Yashoda. If you bring Krishna a little fame, He in turn brings you lots of fame.

The second reason for enacting the Damodar Lila was to establish the supremacy of bhakti. Bhakti is a combined outcome of the sadhaka's efforts and Krishna's grace. Most spiritual processes completely depend on the effort of the person practicing. This more often than not, leads to pride of being the doer. But in the process of bhakti, the scope for becoming proud of one's practice is much less since it is not the only exclusive deciding factor. The attitude with which a sadhaka practices the path of bhakti determines whether Krishna's grace descends or not. The Damodar Lila throws light on the intricate dynamics and delicate balance between a sadhaka's effort and Krishna's grace in attaining success in the path of bhakti.

The third most crucial reason behind the enactment of the Damodar Lila was to show the power of a genuinely compassionate devotee's words and the influence those words have on Krishna's decisions. Krishna went out of His way to make Narada's words come true; words spoken by Narada more than 20,000 years ago. Words of ordinary people have the power to influence ordinary minds. But words of extraordinary devotees have the power to influence God's mind. This month long festival celebrates the power of two devotees and their ability to control Krishna's divine mind and body. Yashoda could tie Krishna's divine body and Narada could influence Krishna's divine mind. If this is the power of devotee's words and actions on God, then how much more should we allowing their words to influence our lives?

Understanding the deeper significance of Damodar Lila

The story begins with a choice. Mother Yashoda had the choice of either doing everything herself or getting everything done by others. The norm is to give more importance to getting things done irrespective of who's doing it. When it comes to business, this may hold true. But when it comes to the process of bhakti, more important than just getting things done is the consciousness with which things are getting done. And more importantly, how much can one prioritize serving Krishna by doing things oneself rather than getting things done. We learn this from mother Yashoda.

Rather than getting sweets made by her maids, mother Yashoda decided to make them herself. She wanted Krishna to savor not just the taste of the sweets but rather the love embellishing those sweets. Anyone could have prepared sweets for Krishna but the love ingrained in them would vary according to the consciousness of the person cooking. Yashoda wanted to fill

Krishna not just with eatables but with her love. Krishna Himself longed not for eatables but for love. Yashoda's cooking wasn't just a two-hour affair, but rather a constant meditation. Everything that came into her kitchen and ended on Krishna's dining table had to be simply the best. Thus Yashoda put such unending efforts to get only the best ingredients into the kitchen. Choosing eight out of nine lakh cows wasn't an easy task. Further, arranging special padma-gandha grass for those eight cows to munch on wasn't an easy task. Getting the eighth cow to drink the milk of the seven other cows wasn't an easy task either. Neither was making sure that the milk of that eighth cow alone was used for every milk preparation for Krishna. Who said that bhakti was an easy process? Bhakti is about endeavoring for Krishna's pleasure. Every little thing mattered when it came to serving Krishna. The consciousness of Yashoda wouldn't permit anything less than the best for Krishna. Damodar Lila is a festival celebrating that consciousness.

While mother Yashoda was engaged in cooking and churning the butter, she sang songs that glorified the activities of Krishna. Her goal was to remain absorbed in Krishna all day long. While Krishna was awake and with her, she would serve Him in many ways. While Krishna was asleep or away from her, she would continue to serve Him in different ways. Of those many ways, the most important were by singing (kirtanam) and remembering Him (smaranam). While her hands were churning, her lips were singing and her mind was remembering Krishna's glorious activities. This combination of engaging the body, mind and words in the service of the Lord is called Karma yoga. It is easy to engage the body in the service of the Lord but it is very difficult to ensure that the mind is also equally engaged. Vaishnava sanyasis carry a staff known as tri-danda or three sticks held together. These three sticks represent the sanyasi having dedicated his body, mind and words in the service of the Lord. Though they carry the stick in their hands all the time to remind themselves of this vow of sanyas, it is not easy to factually absorb the mind, body and words all the time in the Lord's service. What is difficult for even exalted sanyasis, mother Yashoda does it effortlessly due to her love for Krishna! It was no coincidence then that mother Yashoda had draped herself in a saffron sari that day!

As mother Yashoda was singing, the churning rod, her earrings, her bangles and her anklets gave musical accompaniment. In Vrindavan, everything has life. In spirituality, having life means having service. Eager to serve in the kirtan, each of the items orchestrated sounds that were in perfect harmony with the melody of the kirtan sung by Yashoda, thus creating a perfect symphony.

As mother Yashoda continued singing in a melodious voice, there was some movement inside the bedroom. She had left Krishna in a transcendental sleep, known as yoga nidra. While immersed in sleep, Krishna was transported internally to the spiritual realm.

The singing of mother Yashoda penetrated the shell of the universe and dragged Him from the spiritual realm forcibly back to His bedroom in Vrindavan. Sleep broken, Krishna got off the bed to crawl towards the kitchen from where the melodious sound of kirtan was drifting.

When a devotee sings Krishna's names and glories, the devotional potency forcibly drags Krishna to make an appearance. Therefore when Narada once asked the Lord what was His permanent address, He said,

> *naham tishtami vaikunte*
> *yogina hridayesu va*
> *yatra gayanti mad bhakta*
> *tatra tistami narada*

"I do not reside in Vaikuntha planets. Neither do I reside in the hearts of the Yogis. Wherever My devotees chant My names, that is where I am situated."

Since Yashoda was singing kirtan, Krishna came there literally on His knees. He loved to see mother Yashoda absorbed in singing with eyes closed. She looked absolutely divine. He so wanted to be in her embrace. But she was so engrossed in singing His glories that she was oblivious to His presence there. Having dragged Him out of His sleep, she had closed her eyes! Krishna snatched the churning rod with one hand and the end of her sari with another hand, to convey a message, "Stop focusing on activities connected to Me and focus on Me."

Krishna was also giving another deeper message by holding that churning rod. The urn that contains yogurt represents the galaxy of Vedic texts and the yogurt inside represents the vast ocean of Vedic knowledge. The churning rod dipped inside represents intelligence. The process of churning represents intense study of Vedic knowledge to extract the essence, represented by the butter that is formed as a result of churning. Similar to the celestial nectar that is formed after churning the milk ocean, nectarine butter is formed after churning the urn of yogurt. Likewise, after churning a plethora of Vedic knowledge, its essence will emerge.

What is that essence? Krishna is trying to tell mother Yashoda, "I am that essence! Why are you wasting time churning, when the result of the churning process is already in front of you? Don't you know that when you churn all the Vedas, I am obtained as the end result? Vedais ca sarvair aham eva vedyo"

Krishna adored His daily routine of waking up to mother Yashoda's loving touch. As soon as He opened His eyes, He would immediately hold on to her to drink her milk. That Diwali morning she was too busy in the kitchen and it was still too early to wake up her darling. Nonetheless, her sweet singing had penetrated the walls of the house to shake Krishna out of His transcendental slumber. As was His habit, He desired to drink mother Yashoda's love that flowed as milk immediately on waking. Stanya-kāma āsādya. He felt incomplete without drinking her milk. His waking up felt incomplete without drinking her milk.

One of Krishna's names is Atmarama, which means that He rejoices in Himself. He does not need anything external to complete His needs. In contrast, a living being is constantly and consistently dependent on external sources to complete its needs. But Krishna is complete and free from any such compulsive needs. How can you complete something that is already complete? The love of His devotee is so important for Him that He is willing to relinquish certain qualities that He possesses to prioritize and experience more of that love.

The first quality that He happily relinquishes is that of being an Atmarama. He no longer rejoices in Himself now but is dependent on mother Yashoda's milk for becoming complete.

On noticing Krishna's desperation to experience her love, mother Yashoda dropped the ropes of the churning rod and held out her arms. Krishna ran into her arms. She picked Him and cuddled Him into her lap. Gazing at Krishna's beautiful face with all her love, she allowed Him to suckle her. The intensity of her love rocketed sky-high as she gazed into His mesmerizing eyes. Her love flowed out profusely in rivers of sweet milk. Krishna closed His eyes to immerse Himself completely in savoring the taste of her love. While sitting in the kitchen of Nanda Bhavan, both mother and son were transported into another portal, a new dimension of love where everything else ceased to exist.

While mother and son assimilated each other's love, there was a serious problem brewing in the kitchen. The milk on the stove was getting a panic attack knowing that Krishna is unlimited, His desire for love is unlimited, His mother's ability to love is unlimited, thus her milk is also unlimited and Krishna's ability to drink that milk is also unlimited. If Krishna continued to drink her milk endlessly, there was no scope of him getting a chance to serve Krishna, limited that he was. He figured that his life was as good as useless, not being able to serve Krishna. In order to end his wretched existence, the milk began to boil over which would enable him to jump into the fire. As he was about to jump into the fire, mother Yashoda heard the sound. She immediately dislodged Krishna from her, kept Him on the floor and leapt into the kitchen to save the overflowing milk. Feeding Krishna was a service as was saving the milk. A devotee should have the intelligence to know which service to prioritize at any given point of time amidst the many services that have to be executed.

Bereft of mother Yashoda's milk, Krsna felt despondent. He had hardly begun, when she dropped Him down abruptly to save the milk. He felt overwhelmingly atripta or dissatisfied. One of Krishna's names is Aptakama, one who is self-satisfied. Whenever Krishna needs something, He only has to think about it and His energies go in overdrive to make it happen. For example Nara Narayan Rishi, one of the forms of the Lord once produced apsaras just by rubbing his thighs. Krishna does not need external help to satisfy His desires. He has to simply think and the desire is fulfilled. Whenever He desired mother Yashoda's love, He got it. Whenever she loved Him, He felt such contentment that nothing in the entire creation could equal that. But on this day, she left Him high and dry, right in the middle of it. For most things in the world, Krishna was pleased with little. But when it came to His devotee's love, it was never enough. When mother Yashoda left Him in a rush, He experienced abject helplessness something He had never experienced before. The second quality that He relinquished was that of being an Aptakama or self-satisfied. He was no more a self-satisfied person but rather a dependent person relying heavily on the love of His devotees.

While mother Yashoda was trying to save the boiling milk, Krishna boiled in anger. He saw the irony in Him leaving the ocean of milk in the spiritual realms to be with mother Yashoda only to be forsaken by her to save a few liters of milk! What were a few liters of milk compared to the ocean of milk He had given up? Did she not understand *sarva dharman parityajya mam ekam saranam vraja?* Why could she not give up smaller duties to prioritize the biggest duty of life, which is to serve Krishna?

The more He thought about His mother prioritizing a pot of milk over Him, the more He got worked up. He bit His reddish lips with his dazzling white teeth. Tears welled up His eyes partly as a result of uncontrollable anger and partly triggered by a feeling of helplessness. His limbs quivered in rage. He stomped His feet on the floor, looked here and there, something to vent His anger on. He found a pestle stone hiding in a corner. It was the perfect weapon. He picked it up and aimed at the bottom of the urn of yogurt. After all, this urn was equally responsible for keeping His mother busy and away from Him a few minutes ago.

One of Krishna's names is Trigunatirtha, one who is beyond the influence of the three modes of nature. Every living entity is fully controlled by the three modes of nature, namely sattva guna (or mode of goodness), rajo guna (or mode of passion) and tamo guna (or mode of ignorance). Anger is symptomatic of rajo and tamo guna in a person. When Brighu Muni conducted a test to evaluate greatness, he concluded that only Lord Vishnu was beyond the influence of the tri-gunas, not losing his temper under any circumstance. But the same Supreme Lord was so violently angry in Vrindavan that He was breaking things in a fit of anger. The third quality that Krishna relinquished was that of being Trigunatirtha. When His devotees do not prioritize Him, He gets angry. His anger is an innocent one. Just like a hungry child who gets angry when the mother doesn't pay attention to His needs. Simply to gain the attention of His devotees and be prioritized, Krishna was ready to give up anything including His name and quality of being a self-controlled Trigunathirtha.

Just breaking the urn wasn't enough to subdue Krishna's anger. He wanted to create more mayhem. Something to make His mother understand how upset He was for being let down like that. His mother expected Him to be a sober and obedient child so He would do something that sober and obedient children would never do. But before He could do that, there was a small obstacle He had to deal with. From the broken urn oozed a stream of buttery yogurt forming a puddle that He had to cross first. He wasn't confident if His stride was big enough to cross the puddle.

The same Krishna had incarnated earlier as a dwarf called Vamanadev. Unbelievably, this dwarf had covered the entire universe in one stride. Now the same personality was weary of jumping over a wee little puddle. Gathering all His strength, He made the leap and landed on both His legs right in the middle of the puddle. As He stepped out of the butter puddle, little footprints decorated the floor on His way to the storeroom.

The saga continued as He broke every pot of butter, milk, yogurt and ghee in the storeroom. Splashing all the aqueous ingredients over the walls and windows of the storeroom, Krishna went to a new level of naughtiness. He kept aside one special pot of butter for a particular mission. Having stolen in every house in Vrindavan, He was now stealing in His own house. He ran to the backyard with that pot. He looked here and there, found Himself a dark corner where the little thief began to gobble the tastiest butter in Vrindavan.

One of Krishna's names is Lakshmipati, husband of the goddess of fortune. All the wealth in the material and spiritual worlds is under the influence of Lakshmi. And Lakshmi is the Lord's wife. When someone possesses everything, why would He become a thief and that too in His own house? What so extraordinary could be available in that house which was not available with all the wealth of the three worlds? It was not the softness of butter that attracted Krishna. It was not the taste of the butter that attracted Krishna. It was Love! The love with which that butter was made forced Krishna to become a thief in His own house. Mother Yashoda only gave Him limited quantities of that butter. He wanted unlimited quantity of love filled butter. Thus He stole that which wasn't given to Him enough. He was a love thief. The fourth quality that Krishna relinquished was that of being

Lakshmipati. From Krishna's point of view, the greatest wealth was pure love. Though the opulence of Vrindavan compared to the opulence of Vaikunthalokas was like a lamp compared to the sun, the Vrajvasis had managed to purchase Krishna with the currency of unalloyed love. The weight of the love filled butter pot in Vrindavan was way heavier than the weight of the palaces of gold in Vaikuntha.

Once He had His fill, He stealthily walked into the backyard and gathered a group of monkeys. He threw the butter chunks at the hungry monkeys who were super excited on being invited to a free butter treat. Krishna was ensuring that if breaking the urn and destroying the storeroom did not anger mother Yashoda enough, then this would surely take her to the tipping point. He wanted her to experience the anger that had overpowered Him when she left Him in the lurch. In addition to angering mother Yashoda, He had three additional reasons to feed the monkeys. The first was that He wanted to make fun of mother Yashoda. When the monkeys were full and would refuse to eat anymore, He would mock at the bad quality of butter that she had made which even monkeys refuse to eat. The second reason was that He wanted to offer the monkeys butter as a mark of gratitude for everything they did for Him while He had incarnated as Rama. As Rama, He could not offer them much because He was in exile and without any resources. But as Krishna, He had access to all the butter in Nanda Bhavan. So this was the time to reciprocate. The third reason was that He wanted the monkeys' help to know when mother Yashoda came to catch Him. Monkeys, by nature, are very sensitive to any human approaching them. If mother Yashoda found Him there, the monkeys being alert would react immediately to give Him sufficient time to make a headway.

Meanwhile, mother Yashoda returned and saw the mess Krishna had created. With a stick in her hand, she looked around for Him. It wasn't too difficult to trace Him because He had left a trail of white butter footprints behind. But she was barely prepared for the shock she got when she reached the backyard and saw Her naughty boy seated on a wooden grinding mortar distributing butter freely to the monkeys. Her hours of hard work and effort was being thrown to these insignificant monkeys. She fumed with anger. As soon as Krishna saw fear in the eyes of the monkeys, He turned behind just in time to see His mother rushing towards Him with a raised stick and an angry bird look. Of all the things He had planned, He had not planned for the possibility of her carrying a stick. He knew she would be angry but not to this extent that she would actually hit Him with a stick. Great anxiety captured His small heart that threatened to jump out in fear. In a jiffy, He bounced off the grinding mortar and dashed for dear life. The monkeys ran helter-skelter too. Krishna had never been through this degree of fear. Not even when He confronted dangerous demons! As He ran, the only thing that enveloped His mind was the stick in mother Yashoda's hand. It looked meaner than the meanest of demons.

Copious tears flowed out His eyes. His little limbs trembled. He turned around now and again to see His mother, who evoked dual emotions in Him. Her face evoked sweet love in His heart while her stick evoked terrible fear.

One of Krishna's names is Bhayakrita, which means the giver of fear. Another name is Bhayanaashanah, which means destroyer of fear. Yet another name is Veetabhayah, which means one with no fear. He is also called Bhayapahah, which means one who destroys all fears. The Srimad Bhagavatam says, *yad bhibheti swayam bhayat*, which means that fear personified fears Krishna. Why would someone who is feared by fear personified be fearful Himself?

Vrindavan is a place where Krishna is not interested in exhibiting His Godhood. It's a land where Krishna wants to experience loving emotions at every level and in every way. Since He appeared as a child in Vrindavan, He behaved like one to experience the fullness of all emotions. Had He brought His Godhood with Him here then His experience would have been partial. Thus Krishna followed the law of sweetness, which behooves Him to behave exactly like an ordinary child and experience great fear when His mother chased Him with a stick. The fifth quality that Krishna relinquished was that of being bhayapahah. In Vrindavan, everything increases love. Even fear increases love. When Yashoda saw Krishna in great fear, her love for Krishna only increased manifold. When she saw His eyes following the movement of the stick, her love only increased. When she saw Him rub His tears and smear the mascara, her love multiplied at His heart-breaking innocence. Vrindavan was the only place in creation where fear led to love.

The chase was intense. Mother Yashoda running behind the little fugitive. Though she ran at a great speed and Krishna outran her, the distance between them remained one arm length. No matter how much she tried, she could not reduce the distance between them. No matter how much He tried, He could not increase the distance. The yogis and mystics have tried to catch Krishna in the past. But even after running at the speed of mind for thousands of years, they were nowhere close to Him. Not just the yogis, even powerful demons have tried to capture Krishna. But even they failed miserably. For them, Krishna had not felt the need to run. They couldn't catch Krishna even if He walked. But here was a simple gopi from Vrindavan who was so close to catching Krishna.

Mother Yashoda, out of habit, ordered Him to stop running and being so used to following everything His mother said, Krishna froze for a moment. Yashoda almost caught up with Him but He began to run again. On seeing the greatness of mother Yashoda, the flowers on her hair began to fall at her feet worshipping her achievement. She was about to do something that no yogi or mystic or even great devotees are able to do. She was about to do something that even great demigods with all their powers are unable to fathom. She was about to do something that exalted devotees always aspire to do. Catch Krishna! With one last effort, mother

Yashoda extended herself to grasp Krishna's arm and both of them came to a crashing halt. It took both of them a minute to catch their breath.

One of the names of Krishna is Durdurdharah, one who remains unknown to great yogis. Though the yogis chase Him, try to understand Him and capture Him in their hearts, Krishna remains inaccessible to them. Krishna cannot be known by intelligence, scholarliness or austerities. Fertile brains or clean hearts cannot hold Krishna. Only with simple love can Krishna be captured. Mother Yashoda was not a yogi who did years of austerity. She was not a gyani who studied scriptures thoroughly. She was not a mystic who had acquired great powers. She was not a warrior who could run at great speed. She was a mother who loved with all her heart. Krishna allowed Himself to be caught by the power of that love. The sixth quality that Krishna relinquished was that of being Durdurdharah. Someone who cannot be known by the great, allowed Himself to be known by the simple.

Simplicity of love defeats the complexity of intelligence. While the great yogis try complicated processes to realize and understand Krishna philosophically, mother Yashoda focused on loving Krishna by understanding His needs. Yogis try to satisfy Krishna by following His words written in the scriptures, mother Yashoda tried to satisfy Krishna by following His unspoken words written nowhere. Yashoda understood the language of love in which Krishna preferred to communicate. The language of love has no rules and is purely based on the art of pleasing.

Having caught Krishna, mother Yashoda saw extreme fear in her child's face. What if He harmed Himself in that state of fear and panic? She could not be with Him constantly as she had so many pressing duties to attend to. Thus she decided to tie Him to a wooden grinding mortar. When she tried to use the ribbon in her hair as a rope to tie Krishna, it fell short by two fingers. No matter how many thousands of ropes she brought in, it always fell short exactly by two fingers. The ropes mystically shrank in length, exactly two fingers short. There was a tug of war between Krishna's stubbornness to remain untied and Yashoda's determination to tie Him somehow. This war lasted for an entire day. Finally when Krishna saw His mother completely fatigued after the herculean task that she had undertaken, He felt compassionate towards her and agreed to allow Himself to be bound. The sweat on her forehead invoked compassion in His heart.

The two finger distance highlights the essence of the path of bhakti. The complete secret to the path of devotion is hidden within these two fingers. The Srimad Bhagvatam has the power to present the highest truths in the simplest format. Within innocent looking stories are hidden gems of deep wisdom. To be able to bind Krishna and hold Him in your life, these two fingers are needed. One finger represents the devotee's effort and the second finger represents Krishna's grace. If a devotee puts effort but is deprived of Krishna's grace, the loop does not get completed. And if a devotee has Krishna's grace but avoids putting effort, the loop is still incomplete. Of the two, putting effort is in our hands but getting Krishna's grace is out of our control. Krishna's grace comes only when He is pleased with the quality of the devotee's efforts. Krishna is not pleased simply by performance of bhakti but with the attitude with which bhakti is performed. While ordinary devotees focus on performing bhakti, extraordinary devotees focus on performing bhakti with the right attitude. Krishna was not allowing Himself to be knotted because the effort that was required to please Him was not enough. The more Yashoda put in efforts to bind Krishna, the more pleased He became. When Krishna saw that drop of sweat falling off mother Yashoda's forehead, it indicated the quality of intensity of her desire to please Him. The moment Krishna decided that He was pleased with her effort, the second finger was crossed. The loop was complete, the bhakti knot was tied and Krishna was bound by His mother's love.

One of Krishna's names is Muktaya, the liberated one. Shackles bind everyone in this world. Shackles of desires, fame, wealth, habits and the cycle of birth and death, leave no one free. But Krishna is always liberated and never bound by any of the shackles of the material world. The person who could never be bound had been bound by the ropes of love. The seventh quality that Krishna relinquished was that of being Muktaya. Muktaya, the one who is liberated had become badhaya, the one who is bound. Whom the greatest yogis could not bind, whom the greatest demons could not tie up, a simple gopi from Vrindavan had done it. The knot of love that Yashoda tied around Krishna was not a knot that could be easily undone. Even Krishna's friends tried to untie Him but could not manage to do it. Krishna's belly represents the universe. The entire creation was resting within His belly. The ropes that tied the hair plaits of mother Yashoda bound that unlimited belly. The love of mother Yashoda was so powerful that she could bind the universe with it. The word Damodar means the one who is bound at the belly. Krishna's universe was mother Yashoda. The one who is ever liberated was happy to be bound.

The demigods who were observing the helplessness of Krishna were totally bewildered. He controlled them and His mother so easily controlled Him. While they were wondering about this, Krishna looked up and explained to them the position of His devotee. He was happier being tied by the ropes of mother Yashoda, than receiving elaborate worship in the Vaikuntha loka. As Krishna shared His joy of being tied by His devotee, the demigods got a small glimpse into the heart of the Supreme Lord, which otherwise they had no access to. Within the heart of the Lord were hidden the greatest universal secrets. On this occasion, one of the deepest hidden secrets spilled out of His mouth. The secret of the power of His devotee's love to conquer His body, mind and heart. The secret of the greatness of the path of bhakti that can bind the Supreme Lord helplessly.

Krishna's friends then brought Him food to eat. Immediately after eating, He was ready for more mischief. His eyes set upon the twin Arjuna trees that were in the courtyard of Nanda Bhavan. Crawling up to them with the wooden grinding mortar rolling with Him, Krishna squeezed into the gap between them. But the grinding mortar could not, stuck as it was awkwardly between the trees. As Krishna pulled the grinding mortar, the mortar pushed the trees. Krishna had not touched the trees directly but indirectly through the mortar. He was using the wooden mortar to touch the wooden trees. As soon as Krishna heaved a bit, the two huge trees collapsed. Krishna used wood to cut wood. He destroyed the body of the trees using the body of the mortar. While He was still tied, He managed to give liberation to the two trees. While being bound, He could still free others.

Krishna told the two sons of Kuvera who were trapped in the body of the trees to return to their guru Narada on whose words, He had liberated them. He actually meant that that they did not deserve liberation. But just because Narada had pronounced it, He was forced to liberate them from their shackles. Moreover, He Himself was shackled at present and thus could understand the pain of being tied. By crawling on His knees to reach the trees that were completely out of His way, Krishna emphasized on the importance of the words of a pure devotee. The love of one devotee bound Him in shackles and the love for another devotee dragged Him in spite of the shackles.

One of Krishna's names is Mukunda, one who gives liberation to others. That Mukunda was unable to give Himself mukti, but He continued to give mukti to others. The eighth quality that Krishna relinquished was that of being Mukunda. Krishna continued playing a dual role in Vrindavan. While being a helpless child who desperately needed love, attention and care, He continued exhibiting His Godhood whenever necessary. Carefully hiding His Godhood from those whom He needed unalloyed love from, He exhibited His Godhood to the less deserving. From those He hankers love, He knows that exhibition of Godhood is an inferior experience for them. The Vrajvasis do not want or even need to see His Godhood. For them His innocent childhood is enough. The holy woods of Vrindavan are filled with childhood memories of Krishna, which makes His Godhood less understood.

Krishna loves His childhood experience in Vrindavan so much more over His Godhood experience in Vaikuntha that He is ready to relinquish eight symptoms of Godhood.

- **Godhood Symptom 1:**

He is Atmarama, who rejoices in Himself.

He no longer rejoiced in Himself but was dependent on mother Yashoda's milk for becoming complete.

- **Godhood Symptom 2:**

He is Aptakama, who is self-satisfied.

He was no more a self-satisfied person but rather a dependent person who was highly dependent on the love of His devotees.

- **Godhood Symptom 3:**

He is Trigunatirtha, one who is beyond the influence of the three modes of nature.

When His devotees do not prioritize Him, He is no more a person who is uninfluenced by lower modes but gets extremely angry.

• Godhood Symptom 4:

He is Lakshmipati, one who is the husband of the goddess of fortune.

From Krishna's point of view, the greatest wealth is pure love and not the wealth possessed by Lakshmi. He was no more the wealthiest person in the universe. He wanted to have that wealth that even Lakshmi didn't have.

• Godhood Symptom 5:

He is Bhayapahah, one who destroys all fear.

When His mother lifted a stick in anger, He was no more the person who destroyed all fear. In fact He Himself was in the greatest of fear.

• Godhood Symptom 6:

He is Durdurdharah, unknowable to great yogis. Someone who cannot be known by the great yogis, allowed Himself to be known by the simple. He was no more the person who cannot be known and cannot be caught. His mother knew Him and knew how to catch Him.

- **Godhood Symptom 7:**

He is Muktaya, the liberated one.

He was no more muktaya but had become bhadaya. The one who was ever liberated and never bound was now happy to be bound.

- **Godhood Symptom 8:**

He is Mukunda, one who gives liberation to others. Though He could give liberation to others, He couldn't give liberation to Himself and thus lost entitlement to His name Mukunda.

Damodar Lila begins with Krishna stealing butter but it ends with Krishna stealing our hearts. After stealing, Krishna usually looks for a dark place to hide. What could be darker than our own hearts? At least there is one thing that this dark heart can be used for. To hide Krishna, the butter thief!

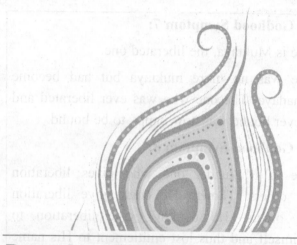

Damodarashtakam - The Prayer

Verse 1

namāmīśvaraṁ saccidānanda-rūpaṁ
lasat-kuṇḍalaṁ gokule bhrāja-mānam
yaśodā-bhiyolūkhalād-dhāvamānaṁ
parāmṛṣṭam atyaṁ tato drutya gopyā

"To the Supreme Lord, whose form is the embodiment of eternal existence, knowledge, and bliss, whose shark-shaped earrings are swinging to and fro, who is beautifully shining in the divine realm of Gokula, who I (due to the offense of breaking the pot of yogurt that His mother was churning into butter and then stealing the butter that was kept hanging from a swing) is quickly running from the woodengrinding mortar in fear of mother Yasoda, but who has been caught from behind by her who ran after Him with greater speed-- to that Supreme Lord, Sri Damodara, I offer my humble obeisances."

Verse 2

rudantaṁ muhur netra-yugmaṁ mṛjantaṁ
karāmbhoja-yugmena sātaṅka-netram
muhuḥ svāsa-kampa-tri-rekhāṅka-kaṇṭha-
sthita-graiva-dāmodaraṁ bhakti-baddham

"Seeing the whipping stick in His mother's hand) He is crying and rubbing His eyes again and again with His two lotus hands. His eyes are filled with fear, and the necklace of pearls around His neck, which is marked with three lines like a conch shell, is shaking because of His quick breathing due to crying. To this Supreme Lord, Sri Damodara, whose belly is bound not with ropes but with His mother's pure love, I offer my humble obeisances."

Verse 3

itīdṛk sva-līlābhir-ānanda-kuṇḍe
sva-ghoṣaṁ nimajjantam-ākhyāpayantam
tadīyeśita-jñeṣu bhaktair-jitat-tvaṁ
punaḥ prema-tas-taṁ śatāvṛtti vande

"By such childhood pastimes as this He is drowning the inhabitants of Gokula in pools of ecstasy, and is revealing to those devotees who are absorbed in knowledge of His supreme majesty and opulence that He is only conquered by devotees whose pure love is imbues with intimacy and is free from all conceptions of awe and reverence. With great love I again offer my obeisances to Lord Damodara hundreds and hundreds of times."

Verse 4

varaṁ deva mokṣaṁ na mokṣāvadhiṁ
vā na cānyaṁ vṛṇe 'haṁ vareśād apīha
idaṁ te vapur nātha gopāla-bālaṁ
sadā me manasy āvirāstāṁ kim anyaiḥ

"O Lord, although You are able to give all kinds of benedictions, I do not pray to You for the boon of impersonal liberation, nor the highest liberation of eternal life in Vaikuntha, nor any other boon (which may be obtained by executing the nine processes of bhakti). O Lord, I simply wish that this form of Yours as Bala Gopala in Vrndavana may ever be manifest in my heart, for what is the use to me of any other boon besides this?"

Verse 5

idaṁ te mukhāmbhojam avyakta nīlair
vṛtaṁ kuntalaiḥ snigdha raktaiś ca gopyā
muhuś cumbitaṁ bimba-raktādharaṁ me
manasy āvirāstām alaṁ lakṣa-lābhaiḥ

"O Lord, this beautiful vision of Your lotus face, which is encircled by locks of soft black hair tinged with red, is kissed again and again by mother Yasoda, and Your lips are reddish like the bimba fruit. May this beautiful vision of Your lotus face be ever manifest in my heart. Thousands and thousands of other benedictions are of no use to me."

Verse 6

namo deva dāmodarānanta viṣṇo
prasīda prabho duḥkha-jālābdhi-magnam
kṛpā-dṛṣṭi-vṛṣṭyāti-dīnaṁ batānu
gṛhāṇeśa mām ajñam edhy akṣi-dṛśyaḥ

"O Supreme Godhead, I offer my obeisances unto You. O Damodara! O Ananta! O Vishnu! O master! O my Lord, be pleased upon me. Alas I am very fallen, by showering Your glance of mercy upon me, who is immersed in an ocean of worldly sorrows, please deliver, O Lord, this poor ignorant fool and become visible to my eyes."

Verse 7

kuverātmajau baddha-mūrtyaiva yadvat
tvayā mocitau bhakti-bhājau kṛtau ca
tathā prema-bhaktiṁ svakāṁ me prayaccha
na mokṣe graho me 'sti dāmodareha

"O Lord Damodara, just as the two sons of Kuvera--Manigriva and Nalakuvara-- were delivered from the curse of Narada, because of which they were like trees and made them into great devotees by You in Your form as a baby tied with rope to a wooden grinding mortar, in the same way, please give to me Your own prema-bhakti. My only longing is for this prema bhakti and have no desire for any kind of liberation."

Verse 8

namas te 'stu dāmne sphurad dīpti-dhāmne
tvadīyodarāyātha viśvasya dhāmne
namo rādhikāyai tvadīya-priyāyai
namo 'nanta-līlāya devāya tubhyam

"O Lord Damodara, I first of all offer my obeisances to Your brilliantly effulgent abode of rope which binds Your belly. Thus, I then offer my obeisances to Your belly, which is the abode of the entire universe. I humbly bow down to Your most beloved Srimati Radharani, and I offer all obeisances to You, the Supreme Lord, who displays unlimited pastimes."

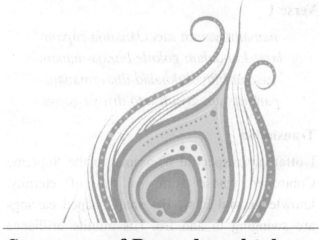

Sweetness of Damodarashtakam

Verse 1

> *namāmīśvaraṁ saccidānanda-rūpaṁ*
> *lasat-kuṇḍalaṁ gokule bhrāja-mānam*
> *yaśodā-bhiyolūkhalād-dhāvamānaṁ*
> *parāmṛṣṭam atyaṁ tato drutya gopyā*

Translation

I offer my respectful obeisance to the Supreme Controller whose form is full of eternity, knowledge and bliss. His shark-shaped earrings are swinging to and fro. His infinite brilliance shines forth in the divine realm of Gokul. In great fear of mother Yashoda, He is quickly running away from the wooden grinding mortar. But she, who ran after Him with greater speed, finally catches him.

Decoding the sweetness

Satyavrat Muni begins his celebrated prayer known as Damodarashtakam using the word namamishwaram. He begins the most intimate and sweet pastime of Krishna with great exhibition of awe and reverence. It serves to alert his readers that although this pastime of Krishna is sweet and playful, it is equally grave and divine. Just because the Vrajvasis had a loving relationship with Krishna, does not mean that ordinary souls could also have that kind of a relationship. The Vrajvasis considered Krishna to be their ordinary child and the child reciprocated with everyone in Vrindavan including His mother in ordinary ways. He even cried! But that does not at all mean we can consider Him to be ordinary. Namami indicates deep respect bordering on reverence. There are many people in this world who deserve respect. The respect that is being offered in this song is not to any random respectable person of this world but to Ishwara, the Supreme Controller.

The Supreme Personality of Godhead has two lakshana or characteristics. The first is the Mukhya lakshana, which means primary characteristics. The second is the Gauna lakhsana, which means secondary characteristics. While awe and reverence constitute the primary characteristics, the secondary characteristics incorporate aspects like beauty, innocence, childish dealings, His pastimes, etc. But the most important aspect of the Supreme Lord is His primary characteristic. Therefore Satyavrat Muni begins his prayer in an authentic fashion by first mentioning the primary feature of the Supreme Lord who is Ishwara.

What is the form of that Supreme Controller? He says it is sat-cid-ananda rupam; a very beautiful form, which is eternal, full of knowledge and full of bliss. This form is not ordinary or mundane. Sat means eternal existence. Krishna exists eternally as a fresh youth who is exquisitely charming. Because Krishna exists, everything else in this world has an existence. Cit means knowledge. That knowledge which manifests itself in the form of all relationships and spiritual emotions. Ananda means unlimited bliss that is ever growing. When sat-cit-ananda are manifest in one combined form then the identity of that form is Sri Krishna.

That beautiful form of the Lord is ornamented. *Lasat kundalam* describes the shark-shaped earrings swinging to and fro, dancing on the cheeks of the Lord. An ornament is normally used to enhance the beauty of the body. Earrings enhance the beauty of ears. But Krishna and His limbs are so exquisitely beautiful and attractive that rather than ornaments beautifying them, they enhance the beauty of the ornaments.

This beautiful Krishna sparkles like a jewel in the necklace of Vrajvasis. *Gokule brajamanam* refers to Krishna exhibiting brilliant pastimes in Gokul the likes of which He has never exhibited anywhere in the history of creation, in any of the universes or in any of His incarnations. The most important factor that differentiates all other pastimes in all other incarnations with that of the pastimes He exhibits in Gokul, is the intensity of love. The mood of the Vrajvasis is not to enjoy Krishna but to serve Krishna. Their entire focus is on expanding the horizon of their service to Krishna. Ready to do anything to serve Krishna. Ready for any sacrifice to please Krishna. They were not simply happy enjoying Krishna's company but ready to come together and protect

Him from any danger, come what may. All the dealings between Krishna and the Vrajvasis displayed intense love.

Even in Yashoda chasing Krishna, her intention was to protect Him. She wanted to punish Him to protect Him. In this world, many times love itself is punishment. But in Gokul, punishment is also love. Yashoda wanted to tie her son because she was worried that if He were left loose, He would hurt Himself. She wanted to tie Him to prevent Him from harming Himself. She ran behind Him and actually managed to catch Him. She not only caught Him but also managed to tie Him. Krishna was happy to be defeated by the love of His devotees. The greatest joy for the Supreme Controller is to be controlled by the love of His devotees. Bhakti is the science of being defeated. *yasodā-bhiyolūkhalād dhāvamānaṁ* essentially denotes that Krsna took pleasure in being defeated. Fear, running and being caught are simply external symptoms of being defeated by the love of Yashoda.

Verse 2

rudantaṁ muhur netra-yugmaṁ mṛjantaṁ
karāmbhoja-yugmena sātaṅka-netram
muhuḥ svāsa-kampa-tri-rekhāṅka-kaṇṭha-
sthita-graiva-dāmodaraṁ bhakti-baddham

Translation

He is crying and rubbing His eyes constantly with both His lotus-like hands. His eyes are filled with great fear. His breathing has become quick. As a result, the necklace of pearls around His neck marked with three lines, begins to quake. His belly is tied not with ropes but with His mother's pure love.

Decoding the sweetness

Fearfulness is a tactic sometimes used by children to save themselves from impending punishment. Krishna being the creator of children is naturally the creator of child psychology also. He knows well that He can avoid getting beaten by His mother if she sees Him fearful of her stick.

rudantaṁ muhur netra-yugmaṁ mṛjantaṁ. When He saw His mother holding a stick, He becomes apprehensive, fearing that she would beat Him. By showing her how afraid He was, He was hoping He could avoid being punished. So He doesn't simply cry but He cries bitterly, rubbing His eyes with His hands. That personality who could fearlessly kill so many demons sent by Kamsa, was crying in front of mother Yashoda, fearing the stick in her hand. Fear personified fears Him and look at what He fears!

Fear itself has various degrees. Bhaya is the first degree of fear and a higher degree of fear is aatanka in sanskrit. *ātanka-netram* means Krishna's eyes were full of aatanka or a superlative degree of fear. Yashoda, a simple gopi with a small stick is creating terror in the heart of Krishna. He is so afraid that His breathing has become rapid and heavy. When Krishna in the form of Mahavishnu breathes out, he also exhales an infinite number of universes from the pores of His body and when He breathes in, He also inhales all those universes, again through the pores. One breath of Mahavishnu lasts for trillions of years on earth. But the same Mahavishnu breathing heavily here is reduced to an ordinary boy only inhaling and exhaling hot air.

dāmodaraṁ bhakti-baddham. Krishna, now known as Damodar from being bound at the belly, is tied not with ropes but with Yashoda's love. The intensity of His mother's desire to tie Him up triggered His compassion that allowed Himself to be tied up. When He saw her tireless effort despite repeated failures, His heart melted and His aishwarya Shakti gave way to madhurya Shakti.

Verse 3

itīdṛk sva-līlābhir-ānanda-kuṇḍe
sva-ghoṣaṁ nimajjantam-ākhyāpayantam
tadīyeśita-jñeṣu bhaktair-jitat-tvaṁ
punaḥ prema-tas-taṁ śatāvṛtti vande

Translation

By such childhood pastimes, He is drowning the inhabitants of Gokul in pools of ecstasy. To

101

those who are equipped with knowledge of His majesty, He wants to show that He can only be won over by pure devotion. With great love I repeatedly offer my obeisance to Lord Damodar hundreds of times.

Decoding the sweetness

This verse talks about why Krishna performed this pastime.

itīdṛk sva-līlābhir-ānanda-kuṇḍe. Through this pastime, He drowns the inhabitants of Vrindavan in pools of ecstasy or *ananda kunde.* He comes into this world only to give everyone an experience of the spiritual world. Pastimes like Damodar Lila are simply a glimpse of what is constantly on in the spiritual world. If this one pastime was enough to drown everyone in so much ecstasy then one can imagine the experience of being submerged in constant waves of such beautiful pastimes.

He declares to the world *sva-ghoṣaṁ nimajjantam-ākhyāpayantam* the secret of Vrindavan. Just as advertisement is needed to sell products by creating demand, Krishna is advertising to lure people into entering the spiritual world through Damodar Lila. More the celebration of Damodar Lila, more is the advertisement for Krsna's product, namely bhakti. Krishna wants the world to know that He is conquered by bhakti. *tadīyeṣita-jñeṣu bhaktair-jitat-tvaṁ*

For any product to sell, there has to be brand recall. What is the brand recall for bhakti? What Krishna uses for advertising this product is a rope. He shows how powerful a product is that can tie even the Supreme Personality of Godhead. *prema-tas-taṁ*, the power of loving devotion.

What kind of bhakti is Krishna advertising here? What kind of bhakti can control Him? He is not talking about bhakti weakened by knowledge of his aishwarya. He is not talking about bhakti weakened by awe and reverence. He is talking about bhakti enriched with prema like that of the Vrajvasis.

Verse 4

varaṁ deva mokṣaṁ na mokṣāvadhiṁ vā
na cānyaṁ vṛṇe 'haṁ vareśād apīha
idaṁ te vapur nātha gopāla-bālaṁ
sadā me manasy āvirāstāṁ kim anyaiḥ

Translation

I do not want the boon of liberation or of residence in the spiritual world or any other boon. Although You have the ability to grant any boon, I only wish that this Bala Gopal form of Yours be ever manifested in my heart. What is the use of any other benediction besides this?

Decoding the sweetness

varaṁ deva mokṣaṁ na mokṣāvadhiṁ vā. This verse talks about the culmination of the process of devotion.

Satyavrata Muni rejects entry into Vaikuntha planets then what to speak of impersonal liberation. *na cānyaṁ vṛṇe 'haṁ vareśād apīha*, not only is he rejecting two types of liberation but also rejecting any other aspiration that the practice of sadhana bhakti can bring forth. Not that these aspirations are small, but his aspiration is much bigger. From a mundane point of view, impersonal liberation, Vaikuntha gamana (entrance) and fringe benefits of the process of sadhana bhakti are the highest aspirations one could attain in this world. But from Satyavrata Muni's point of view, it is *kim anyaih* - what is the use of these three boons? He has found something much higher than those boons that he calls *kim anyaih*.

According to Satyavrata Muni, *idaṁ te vapur nātha gopāla-bālaṁ,* having the vision of Bala Gopal form of Krishna is higher than the highest aspiration. The sage's prayer for inner vision of Bala Gopal shows that such vision is the highest goal to aspire for. Bala Gopal will only appear in the heart as a result of prema-bhakti.

sadā me manasy āvirāstāṁ. For that form to manifest in the heart there has to be intense absorption in Krishna. Whatever one is absorbed in, appears in the heart. When one carries thoughts of Krishna, the same form of the Lord manifests in the heart.

Carrying thoughts of Krishna becomes easily possible when one is in the company of those who carry Krishna constantly in their hearts and in their lives. Vrindavan is a place where everyone is reminding one another about Krishna and helping one another serve Krishna. Only in the company of such Vrajvasis who are constantly carrying Krishna in their hearts will Krishna reflect in our own heart!

Verse 5

idaṁ te mukhāmbhojam avyakta nīlair
vṛtaṁ kuntalaiḥ snigdha raktaiś ca gopyā
muhuś cumbitaṁ bimba-raktādharam me
manasy āvirāstām alaṁ lakṣa-lābhaiḥ

Translation

Your beautiful lotus face that is encircled with blackish-blue locks of soft curly hair with a reddish tinge is kissed repeatedly by mother Yashoda. Your lips are reddish like the color of the bimba fruit. May this attractive vision of Your face be ever etched in my heart. I do not care for millions of other benedictions.

Decoding the sweetness

As soon as Satyavrata Muni began to think of Krishna's form, only one image reflected in the theatre of his heart. The smiling face of Krishna!

idaṁ te mukhāmbhojam avyakta nīlair, the beautiful vision of the lotus face of Krishna. Now even the complete form of Krishna could not hold his attention. In the previous verse, he had wanted to focus on the complete form of Krishna, but in this verse he prefers to zoom into the face of the Lord, Krishna's beautiful smiling lotus like face in close up.

The most beautiful objects in this world appear faded in comparison to the *atyanta nilair* or blackish blue complexion of Krishna's beautiful face. His face alone can satisfy one's eyes. All life long, the eyes had been searching for some beautiful form to rest on. They remained either dissatisfied or achieved momentary satisfaction, until they finally came across the unmatched form of Krishna. Once they fell upon Krishna, the eyes are alaṁ lakṣa-lābhaiḥ they do not want to see anything else now. The original source of all beauty is found in Krishna's smile. It soothes all suffering by radiating the sweet nectar of supreme bliss.

vṛtaṁ kuntalaiḥ snigdha raktaiś ca. Satyavrata Muni says that Krishna's lotus face is encircled by curls of extremely black, soft hair with reddish luster. The word *vṛtam* suggests that those curly locks are like bumblebees buzzing around the lotus flower of His face. *bimba raktādharam*, Krishna's lips are reddish like the bimba fruit. A ripened bimba fruit is extremely soft. But Krishna's bimba fruit like reddish lips are much softer. In the *atyanta nilair*, blackish blue face with *vrtam kuntalaih*, with curls of black soft hair is a pair of *bimba raktādharam*, reddish lips.

This attractive face of Lord Krishna is being kissed by a gopi. Satyavrata Muni fails to specify which gopi, - *gopyā muhuś cumbitam*, kissed again and again by a gopi. He leaves it ambiguous and open to imagination whether this gopi meant mother Yashoda. Since the context is Damodar Lila and mother Yashoda is the protagonist, there is a high probability he is referring to her when he says *gopya*. But he could also be referring to Sri Radha, since this lila also involves Radharani. It was her rope that helps tie Krishna eventually. Therefore Krishna is also called Radha Damodar or the one tied up at the belly by Radha's love in the form of a rope. The sage Satyavrata Muni is so mesmerized by the alluring lotus face of Krishna that he laments the fact that the gopya can kiss Krishna's face again and again, but he has not been given the oportunity to kiss the Lord's face even once. What's worse, not only the gopya kisses Krishna, even the shark-shaped earrings are able to kiss Krishna's cheeks. If mere earrings can kiss Krishna then why can he not have the fortune of kissing Krishna?

me manasy āvirāstām. May that lotus face manifest within my heart again and again. In the previous verse, he had said may the beautiful form of Bala Gopal forever manifest within my heart. However, in this verse he says may only the lotus face manifest in his heart. His greed is progressively increasing. He not only wants to see in his heart the lotus face being kissed by mother Yashoda, but he himself longs to kiss that lotus face now. The present verse reflects an escalation of the intense longing developing within Satyavrata Muni's heart.

In the beginning of Damodarashtakam, Satyavrata Muni was in dasya bhava, a mood of awe and reverence of the Supreme Lord. But now on verse 5, he has reached the vatsalya bhava stage where he is experiencing the bhava that mother Yashoda held towards her son.

Verse 6

namo deva dāmodarānanta viṣṇo
prasīda prabho duḥkha-jālābdhi-magnam
kṛpā-dṛṣṭi-vṛṣṭyāti-dīnaṁ batānu
gṛhāṇeśa māṁ ajñam edhy akṣi-dṛśyaḥ

Translation

I offer my respects, O Supreme Lord! O Damodar! O Ananta! O Vishnu! Be pleased with me O master! I am immersed in an ocean of

worldly sorrows. Please shower Your glance of mercy upon this fallen soul. O Supreme Lord, deliver this ignorant fool and become visible to my eyes.

Decoding the sweetness

This is the boldest verse of the poem. Till now, Satyavrata Muni had not asked for any direct benediction. But he changes tracks in this verse to make a daring request. From wanting Krishna to appear in his mind and heart, he now asks Krishna to appear physically before him.

Before making his request to the Lord, Satyavrata Muni decides that the best way to get it fufilled is by nama-sankirtana, chanting the holy names of the Lord. Therefore he begins the verse by chanting various names of the Lord - Deva, Dāmodar, Ananta, Vishnu, Prabho and Isha.

Deva refers to Krishna being the Supreme Personality of Godhead. Dāmodara refers to Krishna's exceptional quality of bhakta-vatsalyata or deep affection for His devotees.

Due to that special quality, He had agreed to be bound around His waist by His mother. Satyavrata Muni uses this particular title to point out that if the quality of bhakta-vatsalyata exists in Him then it's only fair that He appears before the eyes of His devotees and let them meet Him face to face.

Ananta means the unlimited or endless Lord. Satyavrata Muni is using this analogy for the unending and unlimited nature of Lord's mercy. If Krishna is indeed Ananta, then His mercy towards His devotees should also be ananta. How then can He not bestow His merciful glance on His devotee?

Prabhu is one whose inconceivable potencies are unlimited, astonishing and immensely powerful. By addressing the Lord thus, the sage implies that by the influence of His inconceivable potency, He can become visible to him, even though He is beyond the grasp of the senses. It requires unlimited efforts to see the Lord by one's own efforts. But if the Lord with His inconceivable unlimited potencies agrees to be seen, then one can easily see the Lord with reduced efforts and limited senses.

Isha means supremely independent controller. By using this address, the sage implies that the Lord is an absolutely independent controller and therefore need not rely on anything external to exhibit His mercy. Even to the most unqualified person, He ought to reveal His mercy. What is the use of being an independent controller if His mercy is controlled by intricate rules and regulations that determine who will be an apt recipient of His mercy?

Vishnu means the all-pervasive One. The sage reasons that since He is omnipresent, He will not have any difficulty in travelling a long distance to appear directly before his eyes. Just by wishing, He can make Himself present in front of the sage in an instant. So it's no trouble at all for the Lord.

In short, Satyavrata Muni's sentiments are that the Lord is Ananta, one who is boundless; He is Vishnu, one who is all pervading; He is also Damodara, one who is willing to be bound by

His devotees. Out of affection for His devotees, there is nothing that the Lord will not do. In that case, He should not have any hesitation in appearing in front of a devotee who is desperately hankering to see Him.

prasīda prabho duḥkha-jālābdhi-magnam. O Lord be pleased upon me because I am drowning (*magna*) in an unbroken series (*jāla*) of worldly sorrows (*duḥkha*). Satyavrata Muni says he is miserable, referring to two types of miseries upon him. First is the misery borne simply out of being situated in material existence and second is misery borne out of separation from the Lord and inability to see Him. According to the sage, these miseries are boundless and thus he compares them to an ocean (*abdhi*). Being in such a dire state he calls himself as *ati-dīnam* or very fallen.

The sage begins the verse glorifying the greatness of Krishna and ends the verse by crying about his weakness. This is an ideal combination. Of the most powerful Lord and the most fallen entity. Because he is the most fallen, there is only one way out. gṛhāṇeśa mām ajñam edhy akṣi-dṛśyaḥ is a request for the Lord to deliver the poor ignorant fool that he is, by becoming visible to his eyes. When one makes a request, it shouldn't sound like an order. Therefore he uses the word kṛpā-dṛṣṭi, which means requesting the Lord to deliver him by casting His uninterrupted glance of compassion, which resembles vristya, or downpour of nectar.

Satyavrata Muni prays like this. "O Dāmodara, Your mother has so much affection for You. With profound motherly affection, she cares for You and nurtures You, considering You to be her dependent child. Just as a mother's qualities normally appear in her children, her motherly quality of forgiveness and compassion should also appear in You. If she is so compassionate, surely You being her son, will also be equally compassionate. Therefore, kindly ignore my offences, my sins, my anarthas and my bad qualities, and just be pleased with me. Kindly grant me Your causeless mercy.

In the first and second verse Satyavrata Muni offers obeisance to Damodar, who is controlled by the prema or love of His devotees. In the third verse he offers repeated vandana or prayers unto Damodar. In the fourth and fifth verses, he condemns all the goals of life beginning with mokña, and prays for the Bal Gopal form of Krishna to forever manifest within his heart. Only now, in the sixth verse, is he praying for direct darshan of the Supreme Lord.

The sequence of prayers in this verse is as follows: prasida which means kindly be pleased with me; then is anugrahana which means begging for mercy by the shower of Lord's compassionate glance upon me, completely deliver me from the ocean of sufferings; and then he says edhi akñi-drishyah, please become visible to my eyes.

Satyavrata Muni's hankering began with first praying to the Lord; he then went on to remembering the Lord; then his longing grew to visualize him and finally now it has grown so much that he wants to see the Lord face to face.

Verse 7

kuverātmajau baddha-mūrtyaiva yadvat
tvayā mocitau bhakti-bhājau kṛtau ca
tathā prema-bhaktiṁ svakāṁ me prayaccha
na mokṣe graho me 'sti dāmodareha

Translation

Just like You delivered the two sons of Kuvera from their bondage while Yourself being tied to a grinding mortar, and made them into great devotees. Similarly, please grant upon me Your own loving devotion. I long for this alone and do not want any other kind of liberation, O Damodar.

Decoding the sweetness

In the previous verse, Satyavrata Muni calls himself weak and fallen due to which he feels he deserves the Lord's kṛpa or mercy. In this verse he presents a case study of two people who in the past were more fallen than him and who yet became recipients of the Lord's grace. *kuverātmajau baddha-mūrtyaiva yadvat* suggests that the two sons of Kuvera namely

Nalakuvara and Manigriva who were cursed by Narada were liberated by Krishna who Himself was tied to a mortar. The sons of Kuvera were in the most fallen state. They were drunkards and womanizers. Being cursed by Narada they became trees in Vrindavan. Comparing himself to those two, Satyavrata Muni feels that his case is much stronger since he is much more sober than them.

Krishna not only *tvayā mocitau* or delivered them but also gave them *bhakti-bhājau kṛtau ca* which means they were made into great devotees. Satyavrata Muni is pressing this point now. His demand is if Krishna could make such loafers into lovers of God, then surely he deserves more. Now that he has proof that Krishna does make such exceptions, the sage shares with Lord the exact flavor of devotion that he wants. *tathā prema-bhaktiṁ svakāṁ me prayaccha*, he is very clear that he wants to experience the highest prema or love with which mother Yashoda tied Damodar to the wooden grinding mortar. He doesn't want anything else except this boon. *Na mokshe* which means he has no desire for liberation. In fact he is telling this here just to reiterate that He will not bargain or settle with an inferior boon like moksha.

In the previous verse, Satyavrata Muni had prayed for direct darshan of the Lord. In this verse, he prays to the Lord for *prema-bhakti*. The reason for the change of demand is that the sage begins to realize that if he does get darshan of the Lord once, it would definitely not be enough. His mind would never be satiated with one darshan of the Lord. So he plans a strategy to get repeated darshan of the Lord whenever he wants. Realizing that the sure-shot way of attaining darshan of the Lord is through *prema-bhakti*, now he keeps that attainment of *prema-bhakti* as his goal.

Verse 8

namas te 'stu dāmne sphurad dīpti-dhāmne
tvadīyodarāyātha viśvasya dhāmne
namo rādhikāyai tvadīya-priyāyai
namo 'nanta-līlāya devāya tubhyam

Translation

I first of all offer my obeisance to the celebrated and effulgent rope that binds Your belly. I then offer my obeisance to Your belly which is the abode of the entire universe. I next offer my obeisance to Your most beloved Radhika. I finally offer my obeisance to You, O Supreme Lord, who performs unlimited pastimes.

Decoding the sweetness

namas te 'stu dāmne sphurad dīpti-dhāmne. Satyavrata Muni begins the last verse by saying, "I offer my respectful obeisance to the wondrous rope binding Your waist. It is the abode and refuge of all splendid effulgence." He establishes the fact that the extraordinary rope replete with infinite effulgence was concentrated brahma.

tvadīyodarāyātha viśvasya dhāmne the sage continues, "Next, I offer my obeisance to Your belly because the complete manifestation of Your beauty and Your vātsalya-lélā only manifest when Your belly is bound by the rope. Your belly is the basis of the entire universe consisting of all created beings both moving and nonmoving. In fact, the lotus of the fourteen planetary systems arose from the lotus-like navel in the centre of Your belly." The sage conveys that by binding the belly of Krishna, mother Yashoda had in fact brought the entire cosmos under her control.

This being the last verse of the prayer, Satyavrata Muni wants to make sure that there is no discrepancy in his prayers. If by chance there's any shortcoming in his prayer, he plays safe by naming someone who Krishna loves the most. *namo rādhikāyai tvadīya-priyāyai* which means that he is bowing down to Srimati Radharani, the beloved of Krishna. Only by the mercy of Krishna's loved ones can he attain his cherished goal which normally he cannot even think of attaining. He then adds one more element to seal the deal. *namo 'nanta-līlāya devāya tubhyam* which means that he is offering his respects to the unlimited pastimes of Krishna. He is specifically referring to one pastime which is most dear to Krishna which is the Rasa Lila which he refers to as Ananta Lila since it goes on for a long period and lasts for a night of Brahma. Ananta Lila also means that Krishna has performed unlimited pastimes and he offers respects to all of them.

Initially Satyavrata Muni is only concerned for developing his love for Krishna and nothing else. But by the end of Damodarastakam, he realizes that in order to develop his connection with Krishna, he has to first develop his connection with those intimately connected with Krishna. Thus he ends his prayers by offering his respects to Radharani who is the most beloved devotee of Krishna and to Krishna's pastimes that serve as the greatest awakeners of Krishna prema.

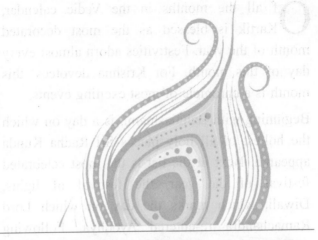

The Glorious Month of Kartik

Of all the months in the Vedic calendar, Kartik is blessed as the most decorated month of the year. Festivities adorn almost every day of this month. For Krishna devotees, this month is a chronicle of most exciting events.

Beginning with Bahulashtami, is a day on which the holiest of all holy places Sri Radha Kunda appeared. Next in the list is the most celebrated festival of the year, the festival of lights, Diwali, which marks the day on which Lord Ramachandra re-entered Ayodhya. Following which is the most glorious festival of Govardhan Puja, reminiscent of Krishna carrying the Govardhan hill for seven days and seven nights. Bhai Dooj or technically Bhrartri Dwitiya, is a festival celebrating brotherhood and sisterhood, commemorating the historic meeting of Yama with his sister Yamuna.

The Kartik month also celebrates the wonderful festival of Gopashtami, the day when Krishna graduated from calf caring to cow caring. The grand Jagadhaatri puja or Durga puja also occurs this month. Lord Vishnu then wakes up from his mystic slumber during Kartik. This occurs on Sri Uthaana Ekadasi which marks the end of Caturmaas, the mystic slumber of Lord Vishnu. The most special Kartik purnima in the month of Kartik is the harbinger of the most auspicious Rasayatra or Rasa dance of Radha and Krishna. Moreover, Kartik purnima is the day on which the Lord appeared as Matsya avatar, the divine fish incarnation to save the Vedas. Also it's the purnima when Lord Shiva killed Tripurasura demon. Next, Vrindadevi, the ultimate manager of Vrindavan and all the pastimes there, celebrates her divine appearance day. It was in Kartik again when Tulsi Shaligram vivaha takes place celebrating the eternal bond of Tulsi devi with Lord Vishnu.

But apart from all these festivals that occur on individual days of the month of Kartik, there is one festival that is celebrated every single day of the month! The above listed festivals find their names in the calendar but this special festival doesn't find itself on the almanac because every day of the month would have to be earmarked to celebrate it. If all other festivals bring joy to the devotees' hearts, this particular festival floods their hearts to make them dance in jubilation. Probably the only festival in the Vaishnava tradition that is celebrated for an entire month is the festival commemorating Damodar Lila. Each pastime of every incarnation of the Lord is celebrated for a day in the year, but if a pastime is celebrated for an entire month, imagine how important it is! The all-pervading nature of the festival is such that Kartik month itself is referred to as Damodar month.

Every month in the Vedic calendar is presided over by a deity. The presiding deity for the month of Kartik is none other than Sri Radharani. The Goswamis refer to Radharani as Kartik devi or goddess of Kartik. In fact the Hari Bhakti Vilas (16/195) says,

tatah priyatama visno radhika gopikasu ca
kartike pujaniya ca sri damodara sannidhau

"Of all the gopis, Sri Radhika is the dearest to Lord Krishna. In the month of Kartik, one should worship Sri Radha along with Sri Damodara."

Specifically referring to the month of Kartik, the Hari Bhakti Vilas has three powerful statements that establish its supremacy.

Hari Bhakti Vilas (16/36) says,

kartika khalu vai masam sarva masesu ca uttamam
punyanam paramam punyam pavananam ca pavanam

"The month of Kartik is considered the topmost of all the months and is the most pious, purifying and auspicious of all months."

Hari Bhakti Vilas (16/39 - 40) says,

na kartika samo maso na krtena samam yugam
na veda sadrsam na tirtha gangaya samam
kartikah pravaro maso vaisnavanam priyah sada
kartikam skalam yastu bhaktya sevate vaisnavah

"Just like there is no yuga like Satya yuga, there is no scripture equal to the Vedas and there is no holy place equal to the Ganga, similarly there is no month equivalent to Kartik. Therefore the Vaishnavas hold the month of Kartik very dear to their heart."

Hari Bhakti Vilas (16/41) says,

dvadasu api masesu kartikah krsna vallabah
tasmin sampujito visnur alpakair apy upayanaih
dadati vaisnavanam lokam iti evam niscitam maya

"Of all the twelve months, the month of Kartik is most dear to Lord Krishna. Anyone offering even a little worship to Him in this month, gets a residence in His own abode."

In the Bhakti Sandharbha (Anuccheda 153), Jiva Goswami quoting from Vishnu Purana, narrates a beautiful story that drives home the impact of just a little worship to Lord Krishna in the month of Kartik. This story is also mentioned in the Skanda Purana and quoted as well by Sanatana Goswami in his Digdarshini-tika. This story emphasizes the greatness of the power of devotion and Krishna's eagerness to reciprocate even when he sees only a trace of devotion in an entity. Although illustrating the power of grace, it is not to be considered a norm but an exception. Such stories are not to be emulated but are rather meant to derive inspiration from.

Chitraratha was the King of Vidharbha. He was blessed with 115 sons and a daughter named Lalitika. Chitraratha gave her hand in marriage to the King of Kashi. Though the king of Kashi had 300 wives, he loved Lalitika so much that he made her his principal queen. Lalitika was a devoted queen, a dutiful wife and a beautiful soul. As much brilliant was her external beauty, that much more was her internal devotion to Lord Hari. From the beginning of the dark half of the month of Asvina (September-October), till the bright half of the month of Kartik (October-November), Lalitika undertook an unusual vow. She ensured that she lit thousands of lamps all day long at the temple of Lord Vishnu.

Not only did she light up the abode of the Lord, she also lit Brahmanas' houses, crossroads, holy trees, mountain tops, entire stretch of bank of the river and even the surface of wells. Everyone was astounded looking at her very unique desire to light up so many lamps painstakingly every single day for an entire month. Her co-wives could not control their curiosity anymore and one day surrounded her to reveal the reasons behind her herculean effort to light up innumerable lamps, especially in and around the temple of Lord Vishnu.

Lalitika smiled. She said it was simply an expression of her gratitude for what she had already received in abundance from the Lord.

The eager faces of her co-wives to hear her story, prompted her to give more details. She began her saga, "My faith in the power of offering lamps to Lord Vishnu during the month of Kartik goes back to my previous life when I was a mouse!"

This intrigued her audience and they hung on to every word she said. She continued narrating the story of faith to her captive audience.

"On the banks of an auspicious river named Umadevi, which flows in the country of Madra, was a holy place named Narasimha. The river was revered to be a conglomeration of waters from all holy places in the world. Anyone who died in that holy abode was said to have achieved the perfection of his or her life, assisted by none other than Parvati, the consort of Lord Shiva.

The place was called Narasimha because after slaying Hiranyakashipu, the half-man, half-lion form of the Lord had taken a dip in that river. Sauvira, a king, had facilitated the construction of a beautiful temple of Lord Vishnu nearby. In that ancient temple, lived a priest who ensured daily worship of the deities. I too happened to be living in some corner of that temple in the body of a female mouse. One Ekadashi evening in the month of Kartik, the lamp offered to Lord Vishnu was on the verge of getting extinguished. Desperately hungry for some food, I found the cotton wick dipped in ghee to be perfect to munch on. Aware of the blazing fire on the other side of the wick, I carefully began to chew from the safe side.

Just as I was enjoying the safe side of the wick, a cat appeared out of nowhere and pounced upon me. Leaping to safety, I sprinted away with the burning wick held between my jaws. Running for dear life, little did I realize that the flame was becoming bigger and bigger fanned by the wind! Soon my body was caught in flames and looked like the burning wick. Fighting for life, I turned around in circles, in a desperate attempt to put off the burning fire. But unfortunately I was charred to death right inside the altar, in front of the deity of Lord Vishnu.

But behind every unfortunate incident, there is always a seed of positivity, as I learnt that day. I was struggling for my dear life and Lord Vishnu was gazing at me. It was His mercy that He took my struggle to mean a self-immolation attempt to make an offering of myself for His pleasure on Ekadashi in the auspicious month of Kartik. Lord Vishnu is so eager to reciprocate that He knowingly accepted my foolishness as devotion. Only to give me an opportunity to continue the little devotional service I had involuntarily begun in the body of a mouse. As a result I found myself born in the body of the daughter of the King of Vidharbha.

Though I had attained a human body, the lesson I learnt in the body of a mouse still remains fresh in my memory. Every single day I recollect with gratitude the Lord's kindness upon me. Every year I wait for the holy month of Kartik to celebrate the mercy that the Lord bestowed on me. Every lamp that I light on each day of Kartik, is simply an offering of my gratitude to the Lord for His grace. If the power of one lamp offered during Kartik can get me a human birth with the fortune to practice pure devotional service, than what could be the power of a millions of lamps offered on every day of Kartik?"

As per the Uttara Khanda (112.3) of the Padma Purana, "Of all months, the month of Kartik is most dear to Me. Of all plants, the Tulsi plant is most dear to Me. Of all places, the holy abode of Dwarka is most dear to Me. Of all days, Ekadashi is most dear to Me."

Having served Lord Vishnu on Ekadashi that occurs in the month of Kartik, the female mouse achieved the perfection of devotion.

Of the numerous devotional services recommended, the topmost is considered to be offering of lamps to Lord Damodar. It is said in the Skanda Purana that when one offers a lamp during the month of Kartik, sins accrued from many millions of births get eradicated within half the time taken to blink an eye! Offering a lamp to the Supreme Lord is equivalent to performing all the Vedic sacrifices and bathing in all the holy rivers. In fact it is said that even if one does not chant any mantras, does not perform any pious deeds and does not have any purity, but simply offers a lamp to Krishna, everything in such a person's life becomes perfect. Not only will this person attain glory and fortune in this life, but also attain the eternal spiritual world at the end of life. If simply offering one lamp in the month of Kartik gets one such immense benefits, one cannot even imagine the result for one who sincerely offers a lamp to the Supreme Lord Damodar for the entire month.

Hari Bhakti Vilas highly recommends one to worship Lord Damodar by loving devotional recitation of the prayer written by Satyavrata muni known as Damodarashtakam along with offering of lamps to the Lord.

Of course, for a genuine devotee of Lord Krishna whose goal is to ultimately develop his love towards the Lord, these external benefits do not really matter. He is not concerned about any glory or fame in this transient material world. He understands that over and beyond these external benefits lies the real intangible benefit of unlocking the hidden Pandora of love of God dormant within the heart. These benefits that are engraved in the ancient scriptures as well as ascertained by the great acaryas are simply sources of inspiration to trigger our spiritually lazy minds into action. Even if it begins by running after small carrots dangling in front of us promising short-term immediate happiness, it will eventually help us build a long term relationship with the Supreme Lord. Each lamp deepens the eternal bond. Each devotional process enhances the bond further. While they may bring us temporary tangible material gains, what one should really focus on is the permanent intangible spiritual bonding that they help create.

In fact great acaryas have considered the month of Kartik to be a habit-forming month. For anything to become a habit, it has to be done consecutively for 21 days. The best and the worst of habits stick onto us when continuously done for three weeks. Kartik is the time to form special devotional habits that can become long-term assets. Even if we develop one special habit in this month of Kartik, that habit would remain ours for an entire lifetime. It's natural to shun away from developing habits that are painstakingly difficult to the extent that we may not even attempt to do it. Fully cognizant of the mindset of the spiritually backward people of this age, the great acaryas and the ancient texts recommend very simple habits in this month of Kartik. Offering a lamp every day to Krishna is probably the simplest of activities that one can do. Doesn't take much effort to do that. Offering malati flowers to the Supreme Lord in the month of Kartik, doesn't take much effort. Chanting the holy names of the Krishna doesn't take much effort. Anyone who happily and sincerely carries out these seemingly simple activities for the entire month of Kartik, develops a habit that lasts for a life time. Let us thus allow the wisdom of the great teachers of the past to guide us in developing the best of spiritual habits in the habit-forming month of Kartik. Just like Krishna tricked the gopis of Vrindavan with a single desire of stealing their hearts, similarly the acaryas trick us with the single desire of stealing our hearts and offering them at the lotus feet of Lord Krishna, our eternal master.

Author Profile

Shubha Vilas das holds a degree in Electronic Engineering as well as a degree in specialized field of patent law. After a brief stint with the corporate world, he chose to leave mainstream society to live a life of contemplation, deep studies and interpretation of Vedic Scriptures. He went on to join ISKCON, becoming a monk, a spiritual seeker and a preacher.

Associated with Sri Sri Radha Gopinath Temple, Mumbai, he has served in various leadership roles in congregational development and management. He is head of Iskcon Goa, where the congregation has been on a steady growth curve under his leadership. He heads Tulsi Books, a publishing house for spiritual books. A preacher par excellence, he assists preaching programs in Iskcon temples across the world including Mauritius, Australia, South Africa, USA, UK, Europe, Bahrain, UAE to name a few. Pioneer of Gita Champions League (GCL), now an international competition to promote Gita learning in schools.

After 11 years of monk hood, he once again set out on a mission to fulfill the objective of his life. He considers the whole world his home and works with Individuals, Youth, Corporates, Institutes, and Governments around the world through exclusive workshops, seminars, training modules, and learning retreats.

As an author, writing books is an extension of his deep sense of responsibility towards society. He began with the monumental task of writing a series of books on Ramayana. Since then he's written best sellers in succession on a wide range of subjects. Apart from his book series 'Ramayana - The Game of Life', he has also authored the best-seller 'Open-Eyed Meditations' and 'The Chronicles of Hanuman' an engaging and inspiring saga of the Monkey God. His latest release is "Perfect Love', a collection of 6 scintillating stories from the scriptures that inspire lasting relationships in the modern age.